THE ART OF
THE STRAIN

WRITTEN BY **ROBERT ABELE**

FOREWORD BY **GUILLERMO DEL TORO**

TITAN BOOKS

An Insight Editions Book

CONTENTS

FOREWORD

I STARTED TO THINK ABOUT VAMPIRISM when I was very, very young. I think it was a passage in *Varney the Vampire*, "The Dreadful Visitor," that captured my juvenile attention. That and the small book *Vampiros Vivos, Vampiros Muertos*, which anthologized vampire lore from many countries and religions. These books made me wonder for the first time: *What if they are real? Where do they come from?* Part of me started to believe that vampires as a myth were a construct of our ancestral memories of cannibalism. Dealing with such a taboo in a sedentary, tribal community needed an explanation, a bit of lore, to make our collective memories and nightmares manageable.

At nineteen, I started working for my father, and at twenty-one, I was in charge of a failed real estate company he had started. Part of my duty was to sell the excess inventory of apartments he had built before my arrival. He gave me no money, so I could have no employees—I was manager, contractor, and salesman. It was in this latter capacity that I found myself sitting at a measly sales desk (a picnic table, really) in a highly undesirable condo development my father had deemed a good investment. My afternoons were incredibly boring and, thus, I decided to read all I could get my hands on about vampiric lore. At that time, only a few titles were available in Spanish—mostly Anthony Masters, shreds of Calmet, and a few crackpot essays about vampirism and its social and religious analogies.

The value of this free time was that, between the occasional clients, I started keeping detailed notes about the phenomenon. These notes included my own strange conclusions about possible vampiric biology. I came to regard vampirism as a form of systemic, sentient cancer. I remembered a tree that grew in the south of Mexico—a parasite tree that grew around healthy ones and strangled them and drank their sap until the original trees died and the parasite took over entirely.

Through the years, my many notes made their way into *Cronos*, were reworked for *Blade II*, and finally made it into a "bible" for a TV pitch called *The Strain*. I pitched it at Fox and made sure to underline the idea of vampirism as a virus above all else. They passed.

I decided to try to write it as a book and looked for a writing partner—not a ghostwriter but an honest-to-God partner—and found one in Chuck Hogan. I was very impressed by Chuck's *Prince of Thieves* (later filmed as *The Town* by Ben Affleck), and he was quite taken by my ideas, so we co-wrote the first book on a handshake. I wrote some chapters and Chuck wrote others, and then we traded them and edited each other. Much to my surprise, Chuck came up with some of the most gruesome ideas in the book, but, in the process, he also came up with one of the best characters: Vasiliy Fet. We wrote three books together and each of them climbed further in the top ten of the *New York Times* best-seller list. Now TV networks were interested.

We started to adapt it as a comic book series first. I personally handpicked who I wanted for it: artist, writer, and even the cover artist. I thought the graphic novels would be a great "testing ground" for translating the books to a visual medium. In all honesty, the result exceeded my expectations and, in many ways, it taught us how to do things, rather than the other way around. The series spawned new ideas and discarded others that had been key to the previous incarnation of the tale. It was a primer on letting the world we had created evolve into something new. I will be eternally grateful to David Lapham, Mike Huddleston, Dan Jackson, and E.M. Gist and to our fearless editors at Dark Horse. We, in fact, took the notion of "the wattle" (read on!) from the comics and repurposed it upon embarking into the TV series adventure.

Of all the places that wanted *The Strain* TV series, FX impressed us the most: John Landgraf had read and absorbed all three novels in one weekend. His questions and depth of knowledge amazed producer Carlton Cuse, Chuck, and myself. *The Strain* series had found a home.

During the post-production of *Pacific Rim*, I started pre-production duties on *The Strain* with my core group of designers—a group of four or five artists who were lodged a few feet away from my editing room to codify with me the color palette and visual quirks of this world. That is the usual way I work: a small group working for a long, long time. Given the budget and time constraints of TV, we knew we had to plan everything as perfectly as possible: VFX, puppetry, set construction, etc., in order to maximize our resources. I wanted to direct the pilot but had less than one-fifth of the time that I usually get to shoot a feature. Nevertheless I had to deliver a seventy-five- to eighty-minute narrative—essentially a TV movie. We marshaled all resources and went at it. Most of that process and more—much more—is consigned to this volume. By now, *The Strain* has entered its third season under the guidance of Carlton Cuse. I suspect you like the show enough to have taken the leap of faith needed to buy the book. You may be looking for more of a behind-the-scenes peek. And that you will get.

I hope you enjoy it and stay with us until the bitter end with these stories. Read the books, why don't you? And if you already did—read the graphic novels. And, of course, enjoy the show—each of the incarnations is different enough and interesting enough to hold its own.

I thank you—and I marvel at the sick images that came into my head all that time ago, sitting at a picnic table in an empty, for sale, condo building.

Guillermo del Toro
Agoura Hills, CA, 2015

* If you love "meee," make 'er bleed"
* EL A/B/C del plan Quiroga.
* El h. de la aguja → CRISTO.
* Todo mundo habla de lo malo
  del Diablo, todo lo malo Dios.
* El es i hombre de Dios † / Pata d' cabra
  y yo soy el diablo virgen, pura ambo
* Ella es el diablo/de el diablo.
* CITY IN FIRE 1912.
* SAMURAI (police story)
* "How TOASTER VR v. GOMES" Ejercicio Dedo
* PROOF: move earlier
* "I... you... I love your... The way
you dress the way... your hubcaps...
* Alguien muy enamorado le dice al
objeto de su amor: (a quien sólo
  le interesa "X") Confío
  en ti y quiero que
  estemos juntos pero
  no te "X" (o algo así).
  (Ella —o él— dicen "Sí").
    o un "ajá"
      muy simple/casual.
  Ⓐ Al abrir la
  boca y proyectar la
  lengua, un pequeño
  aguijón se sale del
  interior y secreta líquido.

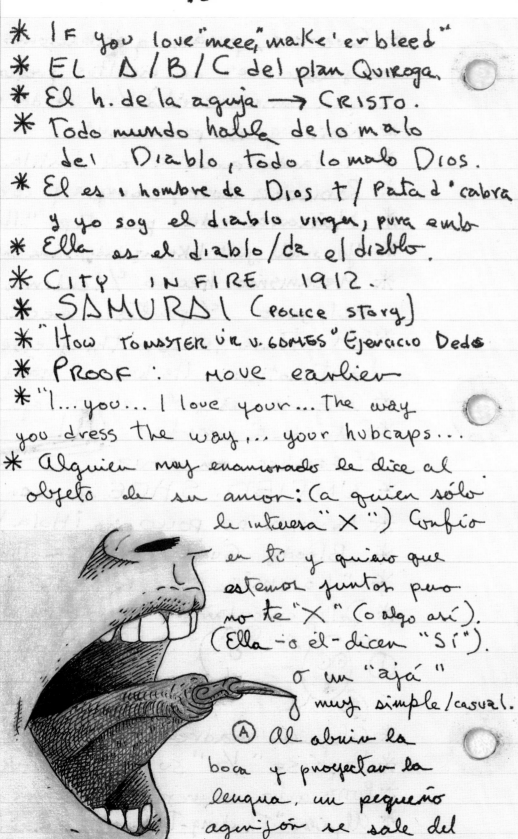

① Brazo Extendido.

② Puño gira
brazo se
encoge.

Muñeca
cambia de
posición.

"Gozne"
Natural en
lugar
del codo
humano
común.

③ Pupila activa membrana
Reptiliana.
en ojo.

Al dilatarse
la pupila
sube un
segundo
párpado

* A alguien le cuentan algo trágico
de su peor enemigo y al estar solo: "THAT'S NICE"

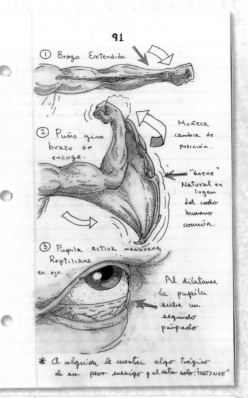

* Ya teniendo todos los elementos
  P/pensar lo contrario escuchamos
  una conversación telefónica (solo un
  lado) y TODO en doble sentido (alguien escucha)
* Alguien OPINA TODO el tiempo mal de
  los NATIVOS de algún país y de su país.
* tumor o corazón
  parasitario
  que opera
  al lado
  opuesto
  del
  corazón
  normal.
  Su
  estructura
  es modular
  o "NODULAR"
* Al "dar"
  con un plan sucio, un "foulplay"
  se dicen: "it must be an error no doubt"
  y después de mucho pensarlo: "... no doubt"
* Niños jugando en las olas de espaldas.
* Alguien que conoció a ARTEAGA y
  se burla de él, nos "REVELS" su pasado.
* Objeto enterrado en pecho, al jalarlo, sale el pecho.
* Le "deja" (hereda) a Ernie la "llave"
  con la que se opera todo en el M/u
* Ernie: Beso y dessays.

THIS PAGE Guillermo del Toro's personal
journals showcase his early interest in
the anatomy of vampires.

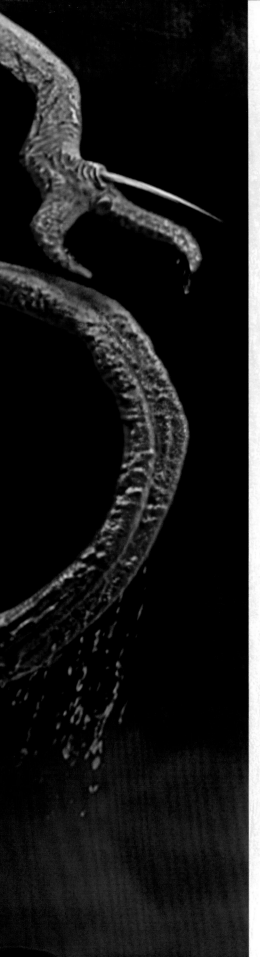

INTRODUCTION

GUILLERMO DEL TORO MAY NEVER have been bitten by a vampire (as far as we know), but this master film-maker's body of work has unquestionably born the marks of the mythical creature's long-standing grip on him. It's there in his breakthrough feature debut *Cronos*—with its crafty combination of Mexican melodrama and bloodthirsty addiction—and in the exhilarating *Blade II*, proof that a vampire movie can be adrenaline-pumping and horrifying in equal measure.

Both those films incorporated ideas about vampirism del Toro had been recording and keeping since he was a horror-obsessed teenager. Drawn to folklore at a very early age, del Toro devoured vampire books from around the world. Not just the classic tales, like Bram Stoker's *Dracula*, that lay down the framework for the modern era's vampire lore, but idiosyncratic histories, ruminations, and fiction from believers and storytellers alike: the pulpy thrill of Bernhardt J. Hurwood's books, clergyman/author Montague Summers's 1920s tome *The Vampire: His Kith and Kin*, and Anthony Masters's comprehensive cultural rundown *Natural History of the Vampire*.

Whether these works took his imagination to decadent noblemen in Eastern Europe or the feasting female bloodsuckers of southeastern Asia, the young del Toro made a record of the reveries these books inspired, going so far as to draw what he calls "musings" on a vampire's physical makeup. If vampires were humans transformed, what exactly happened?

"What would they look like inside?" he remembers thinking. "How would they change? The only thing that didn't make much sense to me was: If they were transformed so thoroughly, why do they have two little [pointy] canines?"

The nature fanatic in del Toro (he is an amateur entomologist) also knew that no species existed with hollow fangs for sucking blood. There had to be something tongue-like. But what would that look like? "Perhaps a mosquito? Or a bee?" says del Toro. "You can certainly find a huge number of blood-feeding parasites in the insect world. And that's where I drew my inspiration from. After all, the strigoi [the Romanian designation appropriated for the vampires in *The Strain*] is described in lore as having a 'bee-like stinger' under the tongue."

The ultimate goal was to create a biologically true picture of an "accurate" vampire, something that would give the process of "turning"—being bit and becoming a vampire—a kind of grimly rational metaphoric logic. To del Toro, vampires weren't solely the province of gothic yarns, figures embodying desire, death, and romantic misery. They were, on the most basic level, parasites, spreaders of a most apocalyptic disease. And if they couldn't be stopped, what would happen to humanity?

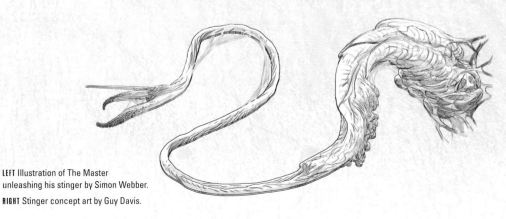

LEFT Illustration of The Master unleashing his stinger by Simon Webber.

RIGHT Stinger concept art by Guy Davis.

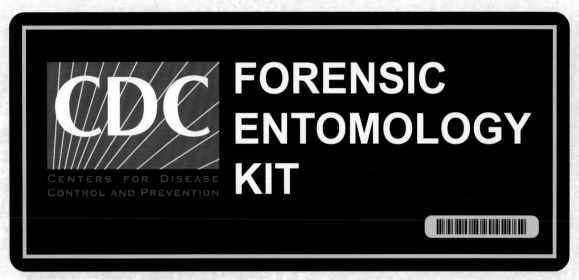

CDC FORENSIC ENTOMOLOGY KIT

CENTERS FOR DISEASE
CONTROL AND PREVENTION

The notion of a fascist regime run by vampires percolated in del Toro's brain. (It was even briefly his movie pitch for the third *Blade* film.) The history of our own species certainly offered plenty of disquieting examples of abominable human behavior during times of crisis. What fascinated del Toro was how completely inhuman we can become during a time of war and how blindly people can be made to follow the most monstrous of leaders. For him, the impulse to survive isn't enough of a moral imperative.

"That's not an alibi or a justification to say, 'Well, I gotta stay alive, don't I?'" he says. "That's the worst crime I can think of: seeing self-preservation as a token of conviction. Our lives are there to be spent, one way or another, for the right causes."

Those familiar with del Toro's penchant for narrative bleakness probably wouldn't be shocked to hear that he believes it would take only a few days for polite society to devolve into brutality when faced with an extinction-level event. Del Toro cites, of all things, his experiences on Los Angeles freeways as just one example: "You could be Albert Schweitzer or Mother Teresa of Calcutta, but it takes almost nothing—looking at someone the wrong way—for somebody to shoot you or stab you, even if they don't know who you are!"

As a storyteller, del Toro has always been fascinated by situations in which the good in a character's nature is tested. People like to think they will behave rationally and honorably when evil intrudes in their lives, but del Toro knows this is ultimately a choice to make, not a simple instinct. When his father was kidnapped in his native Mexico in 1998, the distraught del Toro was faced with just such a choice. "I never gave in to the savage impulses that were offered as solutions," says the director, who turned to hostage negotiators to secure his father's eventual release. "I never devolved into a bloodthirsty caveman. But that doesn't mean I'm impervious to that. If my daughters' or wife's life was in danger, I'm not sure how I would react."

At the heart of the threat the vampire poses is the chilling notion that through vicious, violent contact, the creature changes us and makes us less human. It's a primal act that has frequently been described in sexual terms. Vampire mythology has been ruled over the last couple of centuries by a Byronic model: the European-born image of a dark-souled, seductive man, cultured and craving, preying on young females, yet no stranger to the trappings of society. It's Bela Lugosi; it's Christopher Lee; it's Lestat—all the way up to the beautiful brooding teens of *Twilight*.

But if del Toro was going to revisit the vampire legend, armed with a view of these creatures as more contagious than sensual, there had to be a harder truth behind the fear of something out for our blood, the disreputable allure for immortality, and the abrupt breakdown of a society facing a terrifying epidemic: Who would harness the power of the vampire? How might it be used? How could it spread? And, lastly, who would stop it?

TOP CDC label created by Jason Graham from *The Strain*'s art department.

RIGHT The Master prowling the Boeing 777, keyframe by Keith Thompson with Guy Davis.

FOLLOWING PAGES Strigoi keyframe by Keith Thompson, Guy Davis, and Rustam Hasanov.

A VIRAL IDEA

To bring an artistic notion to the screen, its creator must be an expert steward, and an even stronger communicator if the show is to eventually captivate millions. With the concept for *The Strain*, Guillermo del Toro not only had a convincing, modern new take on a classic horror myth but a truly expansive vision for telling that tale across many long-form storytelling platforms. It was only a matter of time, then, before this master of macabre was able to roll camera on television's eeriest, most ambitious vampire saga yet.

INCUBATION
STORY ORIGINS

WHEN GUILLERMO DEL TORO FINISHED mapping out his long-gestating vampire saga in 2006, it didn't feel like a movie to him. His nasty, ugly bloodsuckers, led by a centuries-old vampire hell-bent on decimating the world, wouldn't be friendly enough to satisfy a Hollywood moviemaking machine too often committed to pulling in the widest possible audience. Besides, to get everything into the story he envisioned, del Toro would have to make five movies: His epic narrative, which presented the spread of vampirism as a global epidemic, would cover several years and feature a raft of characters good, bad, and in-between. Meanwhile, in the years since del Toro had made his name as a film director, television had rapidly become a storytelling medium taking big chances with tough, adult material and larger canvases. He was attracted to the possibilities.

"I was very much taken by long-arc structure," says del Toro. "I was hooked on *The Wire* and *The Sopranos*." Convinced that television was the playground in which to experiment with his desire to go deeper—"to lose [myself] tonally," he says—del Toro felt that the right pitch to the right network could bring genuinely terrifying episodic horror to television. The aim was to achieve this in a manner that satisfied the darker aspects of his narrative while giving viewers a thrill ride week after week. There was even an element of the classic procedural crime show to his tale that reflected the best of television at that time, demonstrated in the way the characters apply current-day science, forensics, and investigative work to solve the mysterious outbreak they face. Del Toro also liked the notion of starting his saga with a group of characters whose true nature was undetermined, allowing heroes to emerge unexpectedly at different times as the breadth of the narrative expanded.

When the initial network response to del Toro's television pitch wasn't exactly encouraging, he regrouped, concluding that the best way to introduce his reworking of the vampire mythos was in the form of a series of novels. And he reasoned that if the books captured readers' imaginations, networks might then be more amenable to making the TV series he originally planned.

Looking for a writer to help him realize his vision, del Toro turned to Chuck Hogan, a Hammett Award–winning crime novelist whose edgy urban thrillers about cops and criminals appealed to del Toro's belief that his concept should combine horror elements with a suspenseful procedural vibe. That fall, literary agent Richard Abate sent Hogan the filmmaker's twelve-page, double-spaced outline for what would be called *The Strain*. "I only needed to read a page and a half, and I just flipped for it," recalls Hogan. "I thought it was great. Guillermo and I met at the New York Film Festival, where he was showing *Pan's Labyrinth* a few months before it came out, and we had a long breakfast—the first of many—and as he went more into detail about the story, I was completely sold. What really clicked for me was the ancient and the modern colliding."

Del Toro made it clear that he didn't want a ghostwriter, someone who did all the work for him. He wanted a *collaborator*. "What I offered was to actually infringe each other's prose on our daily lives," says del Toro. "To truly co-write them. Chuck was really generous in doing it, because I said to him, 'Let's do it on a handshake. Let's just verbally agree to do it. If we then go out into the world and sell it, we are very fortunate, and if not, we lost a few months where we had fun.'"

Over a year, with no contracts signed or deals made, the two passed pages back and forth, writing

LEFT The Master in attack mode, keyframe by Keith Thompson.

freely but editing vigorously, shaping this saga of dread into an evocative, streamlined narrative that they both loved. The duo agreed that no publisher would be approached before then. When the first book was finished and del Toro had a chance to digest it all at once, he called Hogan and told him that if the TV show ever materialized, as he hoped, he wanted his coauthor involved. "Guillermo wanted me there, and I was thrilled, obviously," says Hogan.

In 2009, William Morrow published the first novel to critical and commercial applause, hailing the glorious return of a genus of vampire that was purely evil and dangerous, not a trendy metaphor for adolescent longing or sexual hang-ups. *The Strain* set its dominoes tumbling with page-turning ferocity: a 777 arriving at JFK airport carrying a ghostly cabin of (mostly) dead passengers; a secret ploy to get a mysterious coffin out of the terminal and into Manhattan; a Centers for Disease Control (CDC) investigation led by

that initiate the infection process. But there was also an equally scary big-picture component befitting a tale of epic terror, one involving human recruits—including a wealthy industrialist and a desperate street kid—and an eclipse well-timed to facilitate mass conversion.

At the heart of the story was perhaps the most insidious and disturbing consequence of all: that victims curdled into hideous monsters would be drawn to feed on their loved ones. It's a notion del Toro explicitly culled from eastern European folklore about the risen dead. "The vampire in eastern European mythology goes after the closest relatives, and then they all get together to hunt for the people they love," he says. "I think it's part of the medieval fear of contagion. Most of the time, when you catch something contagious and deadly, it comes from people close to you. So I wanted to see love as a vector of infection."

After the first book, del Toro and Hogan were on a roll. The second and third volumes—*The Fall*

earnest epidemiologist Ephraim Goodweather that rapidly takes unexpected turns when the few survivors begin acting very strangely; and elderly pawnbroker Abraham Setrakian's dawning realization that a hidden war is bubbling to the surface and could prove apocalyptic. Is his life-long nemesis, an ancient vampire known as The Master, making his boldest move yet?

Central to the impact of *The Strain* was the notion of a grand scheme initiated by an especially devious vampire overlord. On the ground, the horror was visceral: humans transformed into repellent creatures with projecting stingers that draw life out of their victims while injecting them with bloodworms

and *The Night Eternal*—were released in successive years. All three books were on the top ten *New York Times* best-seller list, and soon after, del Toro and Hogan began overseeing the Dark Horse comic book version scripted by David Lapham and visualized by Mike Huddleston and Dan Jackson. With the potential television series still a goal for del Toro, the comics represented an essential step in the story's evolution. "I thought doing the comic book series was a great training ground for us to be flexible and define how some of the material could live and how some might not survive," explains del Toro. "For example, action in a comic book, action in a novel, and action on a TV series are three

entirely different things. You can write a thrilling scene of someone being chased down a tunnel by a strigoi that lasts for three pages, but you can only sustain that sequence for maybe thirty seconds on a TV show and less than half a page in a comic. That's the type of learning you do. People say a picture is worth a thousand words. It means the moment you put up an image, you abandon nine hundred ninety-nine words."

LEFT AND ABOVE Panels from Volume 1 of *The Strain* graphic novels, art by Mike Huddleston, color by Dan Jackson.

OPPOSITE Cover art by E.M. Gist from *The Strain* graphic novels.

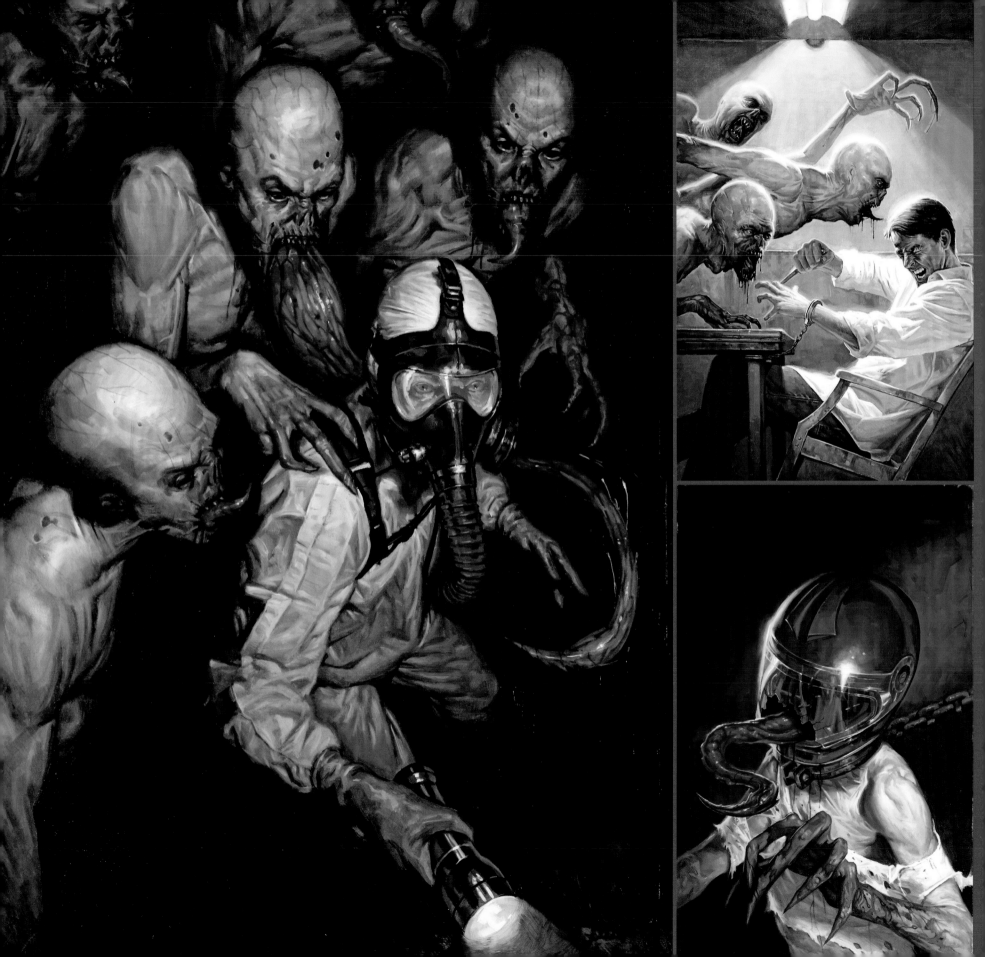

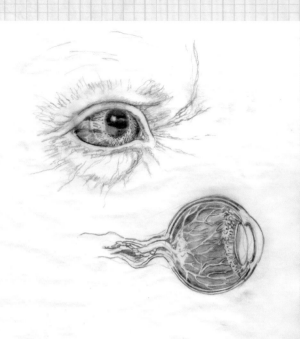

The television world, meanwhile, was catching up and finally proving to be receptive to del Toro's grand, episodic-friendly narrative. In 2012, del Toro met with showrunner Carlton Cuse of *Lost* fame to discuss turning the books into the series he always envisioned. The two immediately hit it off. Cuse had already read *The Strain* as a fan and recalls that the mythology, characters, and narrative arc "activated my storytelling brain. It really upended the vampire genre. I thought there was incredible potential to tell this on television over multiple seasons. I was excited about collaborating with Guillermo, one of the great visualists of our time, because I knew that if I did my job and told good stories, and he did his job creating a compelling, physical world with great creatures, we'd have something really special: a total that was greater than the sum of its parts."

With a pilot commitment from cable network FX, which won the bidding war to adapt *The Strain* as a series, del Toro, Cuse, and Hogan sat down to hash out the structure of the pilot episode. How much of the first book should be utilized to give viewers both a thrilling beginning and a hint of what was to come? Del Toro, who would direct the pilot, knew he wanted to tell the entire story of the airplane—its landing, its grim discoveries, and its menacing stowaway—because it seemed naturally self-contained. Heroes Abraham Setrakian, a professor and Holocaust survivor fashioned after hunters in classic vampire fiction, and epidemiologists Ephraim Goodweather and Nora Martinez

would be introduced. Supervillain The Master and greedy business titan Eldritch Palmer would also get to make their venal presence felt, and a sense of foreboding doom would be firmly established. Before long del Toro, Hogan, and Cuse knew how to end the premier episode. "Driving the coffin across the river felt like a really good conclusion for the pilot," says Cuse. "That was the event that would really kick the series into gear, because The Master has been liberated." One of the reasons del Toro and Cuse went with FX was its filmmaker-friendly reputation and its storytelling acumen. For instance, FX Networks president John Landgraf agreed with del Toro and Cuse that *The Strain* needed to be a finite series and last no more than five seasons in order to give viewers a filler-free, highly charged experience with a definite trajectory. The network also agreed to make a hefty financial commitment before they officially ordered the show so that Cuse could hire a writing staff and start working on mapping out the first season, and del Toro could begin getting the pilot ready and supervising artistic elements—creatures, sets, characters, effects—that needed more time to get right than most television schedules allow.

As the first season's scripts started to come together in an office in Los Angeles, Cuse and

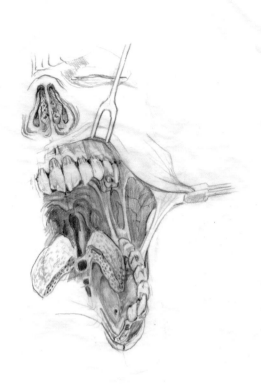

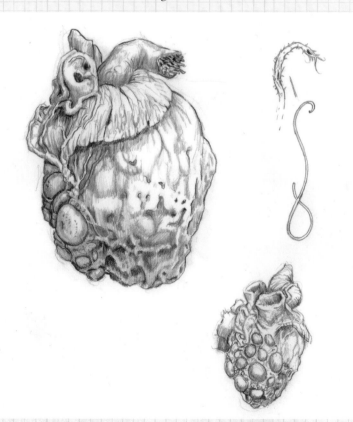

OPPOSITE Cover art by E.M. Gist from *The Strain* graphic novels.

TOP LEFT Strigoi eye and eyeball sketches by Juan Pablo Garcia Tames.

ABOVE Strigoi nose and mouth sketches by Juan Pablo Garcia Tames.

LEFT Drawings of hearts and bloodworms by Juan Pablo Garcia Tames.

BELOW Stinger drawings by Juan Pablo Garcia Tames.

RIGHT Sketches of The Master by Juan Pablo Garcia Tames.

the writers hit upon areas where they could diverge from the first book. The need to give The Master a front-and-center acolyte—a readily hateable villain from week to week—was solved by combining several characters into Thomas Eichhorst, an ex-Nazi vampire. The role of The Master's industrialist partner Eldritch Palmer was beefed up, too, going from wealthy onlooker to more active participant in the fall of New York. Elsewhere, looking to increase the number of major female characters in the series alongside Nora and Eph's wife Kelly, the writers created the role of British hacker Dutch Velders, unwitting pawn in The Master's scheme.

Cuse says the needs of television narrative are more specific than in books: "You can leave room for the audience's imagination in television, but it's a much more explicit visual narrative form than words on a page. There's an ongoing storyline, but each episode has to have a beginning, middle, and end."

One of the new ideas for self-contained episodes that del Toro brought to the TV version of *The Strain* involved an extended vampire onslaught at one location. "I've always wanted to do a set piece that takes place in a convenience store," says del Toro of the notion that would eventually become the eighth episode of the first season. "How crazy would it be that you can be in the middle of a city with cars driving by, and you're being attacked, and nobody would notice?"

The term in television is "bottle episode," one that takes place entirely in a single location and is usually slotted midway through a season to give hardworking art department crews a break from building multiple sets for a week. In "Creatures of

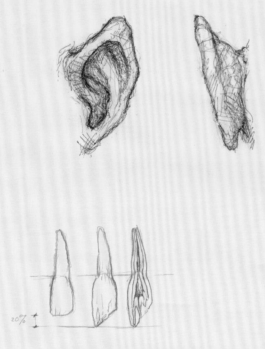

THIS PAGE Sketches of strigoi appendages by Juan Pablo Garcia Tames.

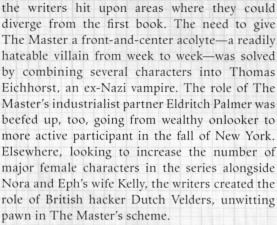

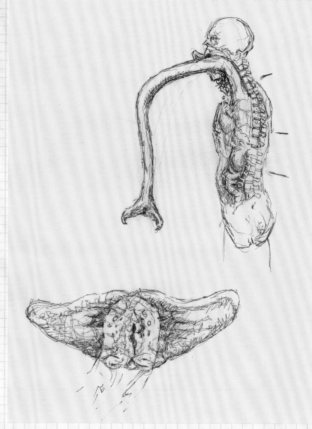

the Night," the vampire-hunting team finds itself trapped in a gas station mini-mart during a strigoi attack. "I tried to do that scene as a set piece on *Blade II*," says del Toro, "but it didn't fit our budget or storyline. Then we tried to put it in the books but couldn't." Fittingly, Hogan was tasked with writing the episode. "Guillermo loved that idea, but it didn't naturally fit into the books, so that was one of the first things we brought up when we were talking about season one," he says. "It was great to be able to scratch off one of our wish list of things [we had wanted to include in the] books."

Speaking about working with Cuse and Hogan, del Toro says it was a winning relationship from the beginning, giving him confidence that his ambitious saga would get the care it needed as it metamorphosed into a weekly hour of television. "The best way to be prepared for any battle is to have really good partners, and that was the first part of it," he says. "Then what you bring to the partnership is what you do best. I come up with crazy, outlandish set pieces or moments, I rejoice when I hear a great storyline, and I support the team by being enthusiastic and creative."

THE ART OF INFECTION

WHEN YOUR MÉTIER IS rendering the fantastic and freaky, getting called into service by a legendary creature creator like Guillermo del Toro is what you live for.

"Whenever Guillermo wants to work with you, it's fun," says lead concept artist Guy Davis, a go-to favorite of del Toro's who had worked with the director on *Pacific Rim* and a handful of other projects. "I never think twice. If Guillermo is going to do *My Dinner with Andre*, it's going to be something monstrous. Something creepy. Something bizarre. I would work on that. He's an amazing visionary."

Being asked to work on *The Strain*, then, was a no-brainer for a monster maven like Davis, who, along with a trusted group of artists—sculptors Simon Lee and David Meng and concept artist/illustrators Keith Thompson, Simon Webber, Francesco Ruiz Velasco, and Rustam Hasanov—came together in a Los Angeles office to turn their talents toward rendering the story's critical visual touchstones. (The office was chosen for its proximity to the Warner Bros. lot where del Toro was finishing post-production on *Pacific Rim*.)

Under del Toro's guidance, a working sense of how the universe of *The Strain* would look—from The Master to vampire stingers and the various character costumes and main locations—would come together over the next few months. Being part of such an early stage in a project appeals to Davis. "In comics, artwork is the final step of the job," he says. "The comics are written, then the art is produced. But in concept art, it's the first step. It's giving it a visual idea Guillermo can point to and then take to the next step of production."

The director is very hands-on when it comes to concept art, overseeing the process as rough sketches lead to fleshed-out drawings and paintings. He doesn't stand over the artists, but he does make frequent visits to okay certain directions or make changes as new inspiration hits him. Giving del Toro choices is paramount, says Davis: "It's not about creating a pretty illustration at the beginning. I like to give him three or four pages, different ideas, so he can say 'No, no, yes, maybe this mixed with that,' and then from there create a tighter pass and then a final pass. We refine it as we go."

TOP CENTER Concept art of stinger organs by Guy Davis.

ABOVE Concept sculpt of stinger by Simon Lee.

LEFT Keyframe of strigoi attack by Francisco Ruiz Velasco.

OPPOSITE Keyframe art of The Master with an imminent victim by Keith Thompson with Guy Davis.

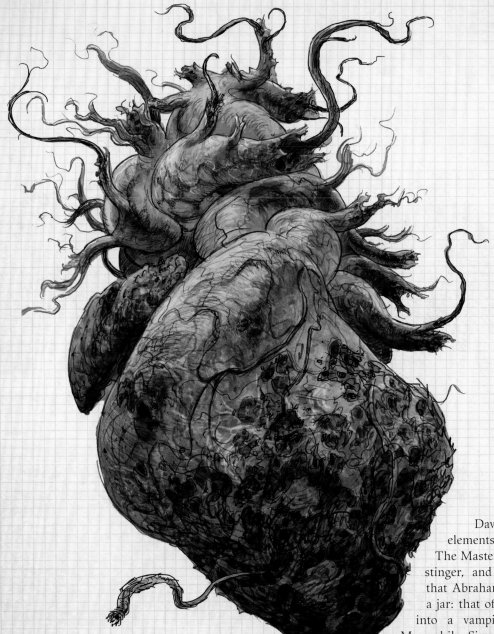

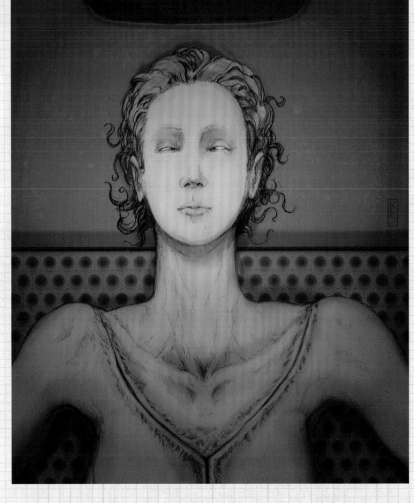

Davis worked on essential elements of the story such as The Master's coffin, the strigoi's stinger, and the pulsating heart that Abraham Setrakian keeps in a jar: that of his late wife, turned into a vampire by The Master. Meanwhile, Simon Lee tackled sculpts of the strigoi's other features, along with The Master and Setrakian's cane sword, the trusty weapon he intends to use to vanquish his nemesis. Velasco, a del Toro regular who first worked for the director on *Hellboy II: The Golden Army*, was tasked with creating key backgrounds that brought various elements together into a painted, scenic whole. These included Setrakian's pawn shop and all its oddities, a vampire attack in a morgue planned for the pilot, and a flashback that depicted the origins of The Master's latest incarnation in a Romanian forest. "On top of visualizing the

moment, it was about designing a color palette for some of the scenes," says Velasco. "They're colors Guillermo likes: cold blue and yellow and green. We help establish that language of color."

As time went on, a camaraderie among the artists developed, ideas were exchanged, and everyone's work began to coalesce into a unified whole. Explains Davis, "If Guillermo likes something Simon's doing as far as The Master's mouth, then I'll use that if I'm doing a design of the stinger, since I need a mouth for it to come out of. We work together, and it's always a pleasure to be a part of his team."

The result after all those months of hard concepting was a series of vividly rendered blueprints from which *The Strain* could be brought to three-dimensional life as actors embodied characters, designers built sets and props, and VFX wizards conjured the fantastical. As a full-bodied production, the television version of *The Strain* was that much closer to going viral.

WITH GUILLERMO DEL TORO AT THE HELM, production started on *The Strain*'s pilot, titled "Night Zero," in September of 2013. All the right elements were in place, but how del Toro approached this first episode would be crucial to setting the scene for the entire season and beyond. Most of the first season's scripts had been drafted by the writing staff based in Los Angeles and overseen by Carlton Cuse. In Toronto, producer J. Miles Dale—who had worked on *Mama* with del Toro—was entrenched as the head of physical production. Thanks to FX's early commitment, departments had been active for months already, creatures had been built, sets had been erected at Pinewood Toronto Studios, and locations around Toronto chosen.

Everything pertaining to *The Strain* ultimately went through del Toro and Cuse, but the show's visual style and general feel started and ended with del Toro. In television, nothing is more crucial to establishing a show's sensibility than getting the pilot right. After that, Cuse and del Toro would be handing the rest of the first season's episodes to a number of directors who would need a clear template to ensure the entire series had a stylistic and thematic unity.

First and foremost, del Toro wanted *The Strain* to feel like a throwback to the horror television of his youth, namely the cult mid-1970s series *Kolchak: The Night Stalker* about intrepid reporter Carl Kolchak (Darren McGavin), whose investigations into bizarre crimes ignored by the authorities led him into a hidden world of supernatural beings and terrifying creatures. Mixing crime drama and horror, the show thrived on an impish reinvention of genre tropes, and del Toro has never forgotten how it felt to be thrilled, amused, and scared by it.

"That was my favorite show, because a lot of the time Kolchak was adorable, but he used to behave in ways that allowed the horror to exist," says del Toro. "You didn't have to justify it in a way that was beyond the universe of the show. You'd wonder why Kolchak was going alone to a junkyard at midnight to kill a zombie without calling the police or even a friend, but that was why I loved it. You had outlandish set pieces and yet nobody was

ATTENTION

CARGO HATCH MUST BE KEPT CLOSED DURING FLIGHT

TOP Airplane investigation keyframe art by Francisco Ruiz Velasco.

aware. It was a great suspension of disbelief. Once the show established those rules, you go with it."

If *The Strain* was going to similarly unleash vampires upon an unsuspecting metropolis, it'd also need to set up an initial tone of mystery and dread. As such, the airport scenes were extremely important, especially the first scenes that show unsuspecting passengers, the sequence ending on a chilling note as The Master erupts from the cargo hold. "I opened with a very classic TV teaser," says del Toro.

Along with terror and suspense, there were other tones del Toro wanted to throw into the mix. For example, during a morgue scene in which the coroner, Bennett, discovers that the deceased 777 passengers are not entirely dead, del Toro has the tune "Sweet Caroline" emanating from a radio as the vampires close in for the kill. "I wanted to let people know that there was humor in the series by implementing Neil Diamond in a particularly brutal scene," he says.

Despite this injection of humor, mere moments later the pilot ends on the eeriest of notes when a grieving father is surprised to see his dead daughter,

a victim of the 777 incident, has returned to him—although her pale, almost translucent skin and dead eyes with their quick, reptilian blink suggest that this reunion will not end happily. All in all, del Toro says, his mission with the pilot was to communicate the show's tonal range. "It was a matter of making the pilot a sampler of the different flavors that I thought the series was going to have," he says. "It had to be a sampler that feels like a unit."

The strict control of color is another tool del Toro employs when establishing a visual language, and, after finding success with the oversaturated hues of *Pacific Rim*, he took a similar approach to working out the color scheme of *The Strain*. "I knew I wanted to direct the series in basically two colors: cyan or blue, and gold," says del Toro. "I was juxtaposing a color that would represent the sun and a color that would represent night. I also knew that we needed to regiment very rigidly the use of the color red so that red became meaningful on a subliminal level for anyone watching the series."

Red was therefore reserved for anyone tied to The Master. Del Toro knew he couldn't change the

ABOVE Eph and Nora find splatters of strigoi excrement on the plane (called "splooge" by crew members on set).

BELOW Keyframe art by Francisco Ruiz Velasco of the CDC team finding stricken passengers.

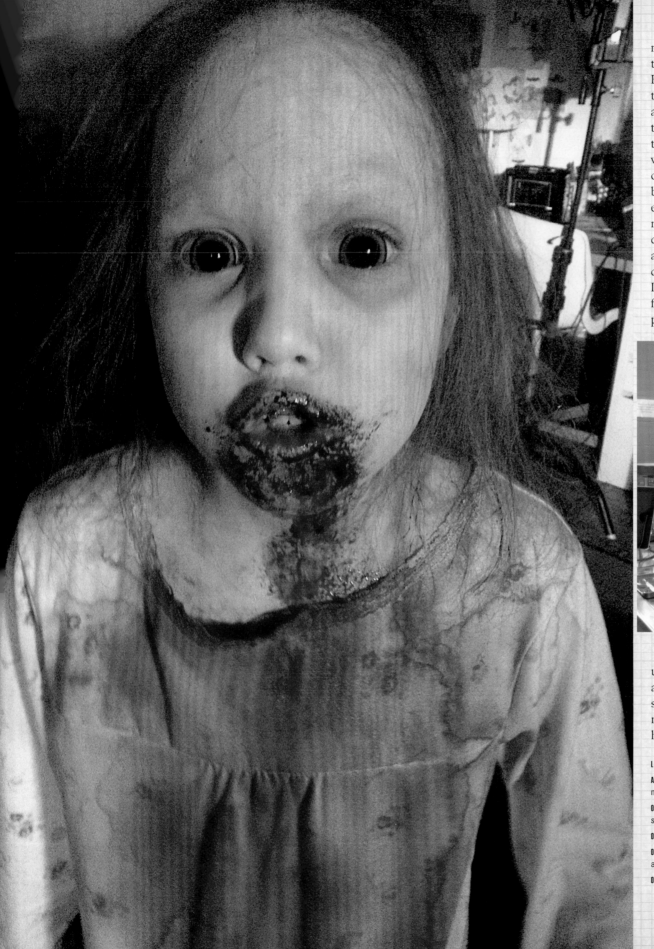

reds encountered in the real world: a glass of wine, the red lights on the backs of cars, a fire extinguisher. But when it came to the dress of specific characters, such as a Nazi swastika worn by The Master's acolyte Thomas Eichhorst, the tie color of the traitorous CDC employee Jim Kent, or the candles in twisted rock star Gabriel Bolivar's bedroom, red was heartily approved. Red was also used liberally, of course, for one other key element of *The Strain*: blood. "I was very careful in not allowing any red elsewhere," says del Toro. "We drove the art department and the wardrobe department crazy. To this day, I do the final color correction on every episode, and each time I do it, I try to take anything that doesn't need to be red and turn it off. Now and then I have to let it go. I'm not going to take out the entire façade of a building because it has red in it. But we pushed a very strict code of colors."

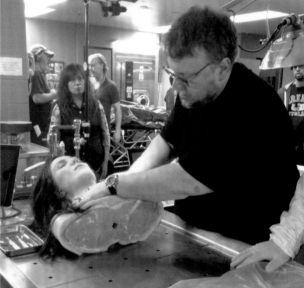

A meticulous director, del Toro believes in the use of storyboards to help refine the flow of VFX and practical work in a given scene, identify the shots he wants, the lenses to use, and the camera movement. Guy Davis was tasked with drawing a handful of storyboards right before shooting on

LEFT Infected Emma (Isabelle Nélisse) in full makeup.

ABOVE Guillermo del Toro examines a sculpted head and shoulders for the morgue scene.

OPPOSITE TOP LEFT An extra with prosthetic organs for the autopsy attack scene in "Night Zero."

OPPOSITE TOP RIGHT A male body cast with synthetic organs.

OPPOSITE BOTTOM LEFT A female head and shoulders cast for the same autopsy scene.

OPPOSITE BOTTOM RIGHT A strigoi extra in full makeup for the morgue scene.

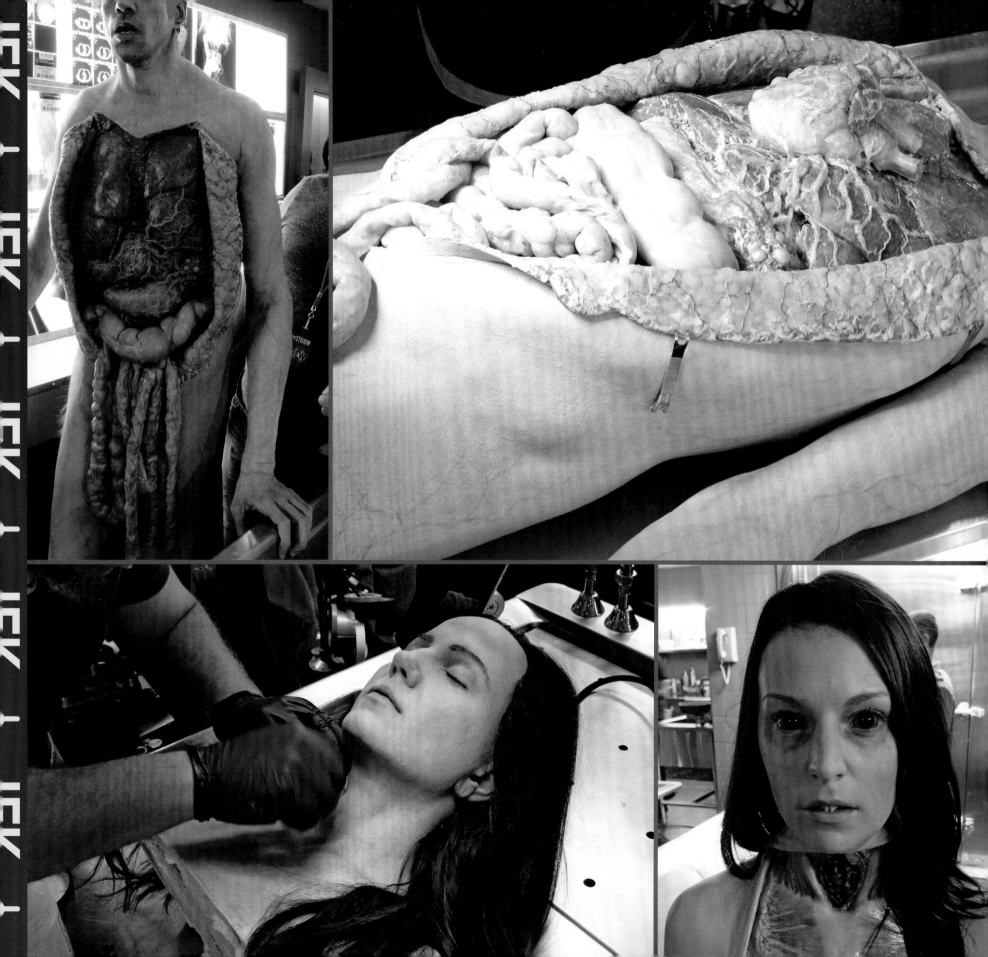

the pilot commenced, based on quick sketches del Toro provided.

"He'd look over the boards each day and add to a scene or change shots if needed," says Davis. One scene in particular, as storyboarded—The Master's killing of air traffic boss Peter Bishop—clearly inspired del Toro to go further. "When we did the storyboards for the killing of Bishop, the scene had Bishop being drained and then killed, with The Master snapping his neck," recalls Davis. "But Guillermo wanted to add The Master actually crushing his head by slamming his palm through it into the ground. It was a great, shocking end, but while drawing it out, I wondered if it would make it into the pilot or be too brutal. So it was awesome to see that the filmed scene was even more brutal—not only did he crush his head once, but he followed through with a couple more hits!"

Over the pilot's twenty-two-day shoot, del Toro expertly laid the groundwork for a series that would feature a wealth of great characters, chilling moments, thrilling supernatural effects, and stylish suspense. Though he was making *The Strain* for television, he didn't let that medium's familiar constraints keep him from creating the most movie-like series he could. "I wanted the camera to move very cinematically," says del Toro. "I didn't want the camera to be constrained by just using camera A, camera B, a long lens, and a

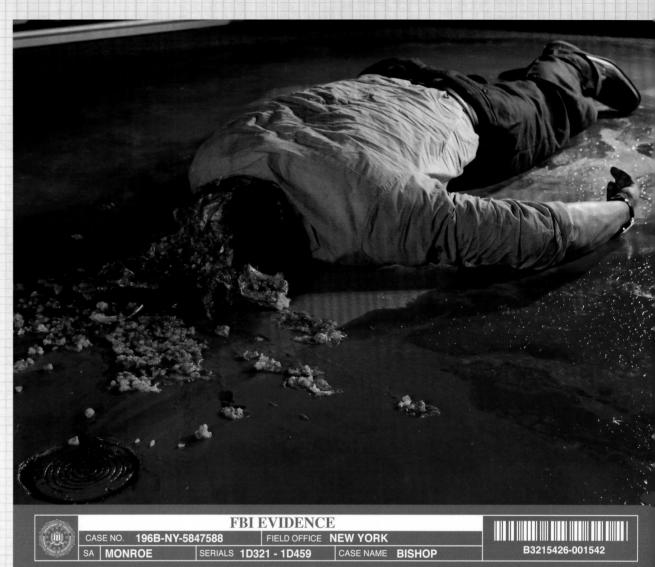

FBI EVIDENCE

CASE NO.	**196B-NY-5847588**		FIELD OFFICE	**NEW YORK**	
SA	**MONROE**	SERIALS	**1D321 - 1D459**	CASE NAME	**BISHOP**

B3215426-001542

OPPOSITE Storyboard sketches by Guy Davis show The Master brutally killing Bishop in the series pilot.

ABOVE AND RIGHT From the pilot, a dummy of Bishop with the head horribly crushed and gray matter visible.

short lens. So I kept moving it as much as possible, as if it was a movie set." Occasionally he'd defer to the judgment of cinematographer Checco Varese, who has plenty of experience with television. "In some instances, Checco would say, 'Look, we only have an hour and it's a dialogue scene, so let's revert to a TV solution,'" says del Toro. "That would come in very handy in curbing my appetite. Checco was my reality compass—constantly reminding me when I could get ambitious and when we could settle for practical."

When del Toro moved on to directing the feature *Crimson Peak* and other directors shot the rest of the season, he was still on board to oversee the series' aesthetic as a whole. "I supervise every single shot in the show," says del Toro. "It goes through me at the end of the day. If you don't like a shot on the show, you can talk to me!"

No one was more impressed and thrilled about kicking off production than Chuck Hogan, who had only known his writing partner one way: through their shared authorship of the books. Visiting the Toronto set of *The Strain* on the first night of production, when an entire city block had been shut down and a huge crane was being readied for a shot, Hogan experienced a new thrill: seeing *The Strain* come to life right before his eyes. "Our pilot was like a movie set," Hogan says. "I'm so used to being on the other side of the cordon with the people watching. All of a sudden I'm sitting right next to Guillermo in front of the monitors, watching it come to life. He has this incredible visual sense, and to see how exacting he was—making sure everything is exactly the way he wants—it felt like I had a front row seat to something really amazing."

THE HUNTERS

THE VAMPIRE-KILLING TEAM tasked with holding back the tide of evil on *The Strain* is a motley crew indeed: a Holocaust survivor hell-bent on vanquishing The Master, two dedicated epidemiologists getting a quick education in a threat beyond their wildest nightmares, a gung-ho pest exterminator eager to apply his trade to the strigoi, and a pair of mercenary types—one streetwise, one tech-wise—who unwittingly aided in spreading the plague but now see a chance to right their wrongs. They're all humanity has to stop this fierce contagion, and, for Cuse, del Toro, and casting director April Webster, putting together a dynamic ensemble cast to portray this ragtag group of heroes was key to the success of the show.

ABRAHAM SETRAKIAN

THE PATIENT LONELINESS OF THE DOGGED vampire hunter—dedicated, righteous, and misunderstood—is one of the hallmarks of vampiric lore, but in Holocaust survivor Abraham Setrakian's case, it's a badge of honor. Already witness to one vanquished attempt to eradicate humans at an extermination camp during World War II, Setrakian has lain low in his unassuming Harlem pawnshop waiting for The Master to make his next move.

As Setrakian migrated from the sternly heroic figure of the books and graphic novels to the series, however, the notion of a flesh-and-blood actor playing him gave producer Carlton Cuse an idea.

"Setrakian is a very classical figure in vampire mythology, which is the wise man," says del Toro. "In *Dracula*, that's Van Helsing. But Carlton brought a very, very fresh take. He reinvented a new edge for him. He said, 'I think Setrakian should be more sociopathic and more dangerous than in the books.' In the books, he's almost a fatherly figure. But Carlton thought we should make him a guy that you love but, because he's a hard-ass, incapable of forgiving. He'll kill anyone of any age, any persuasion, if they've been turned. And that was brilliant, because Carlton essentially elevated Setrakian to the same mythical stature of The Master. He's a force of good as unflinching at spreading good as evil is about spreading evil."

English actor David Bradley, already known for his memorable appearances in the Harry Potter films and *Game of Thrones*, says his version of Setrakian is not immune to fear but rarely feels it due to his remarkable drive to succeed in his mission. "Considering his years, he should be putting his feet up, but in a way, his mission makes him younger than his years," says Bradley. "Which helps enormously, because he has an awful lot of beheading to do."

Corey Stoll, who plays Ephraim Goodweather, calls Bradley as hard a worker as he's ever encountered. "He's like a thirteen-year-old boy in the body of a seventy-something," says Stoll. "It's almost like somebody forgot to tell him he's a grownup. He's often got the worst schedule, and he's never complained once. He's an incredible example to all of us."

Outfitting Bradley to play The Master's long-standing nemesis meant suggesting those long years of living and waiting, living and waiting. Inspired by Setrakian's look in the graphic novels, costume designer Luis Sequeira secured a wardrobe of oversized vintage coats that would be carefully aged and dyed. "We sand it and spray it, so the fibers start to sag, then weigh it down, then fade it out, crinkle it up, uncrinkle it, then lay in some paints and dyes," says Sequeira. "The premise was that he'd been wearing it forever and that he'd lost body mass. The clothes needed to hang off him."

PREVIOUS PAGES Concept art by Rustam Hasanov of vampire hunter Abraham Setrakian's secret workshop.

OPPOSITE A patient warrior, Abraham Setrakian (David Bradley) has waited a long time to vanquish The Master.

TOP LEFT AND ABOVE Costume design ideas for Setrakian drawn by Guy Davis with Rustam Hasanov.

SETRAKIAN'S CANE

Possibly the most memorable prop in the entire series, Abraham Setrakian's cane-sword, once owned by Jusef Sardu, aka The Master, is a metaphor for Setrakian himself: sturdy, purposeful, and hiding a sharp fierceness that ties him forever to the one he's vowed to kill. Plus, the elegant, twisting wolf's head handle neatly symbolizes the hunter inside Setrakian.

The prop master on season one, Jim Murray, knew that getting the cane right was essential for the series. "You identified Setrakian with that piece," says Murray. "When you're working on a show based on books and that has a fan following, you have to be true to what fans expect."

Working from a sculpted plastic version built early on by Simon Lee in Los Angeles, Murray was instructed by del Toro to give the final object real visual heft and so enlisted a cane builder to construct a heavy-weighted, bronze-bladed piece of real beauty. Three of these "hero" props were then built to be used primarily for close-ups that emphasized both the craftsmanship involved and the drama of Setrakian unsheathing his sword at a pivotal moment. These pieces were too heavy to be used for actual fight scenes, so a few stunt versions housing aluminum swords were built as well. For shots that didn't require any fighting, canes without swords were also constructed.

"It's a beautiful, beautiful prop," says Bradley, adding, "I don't think I'll be allowed to take it home with me!"

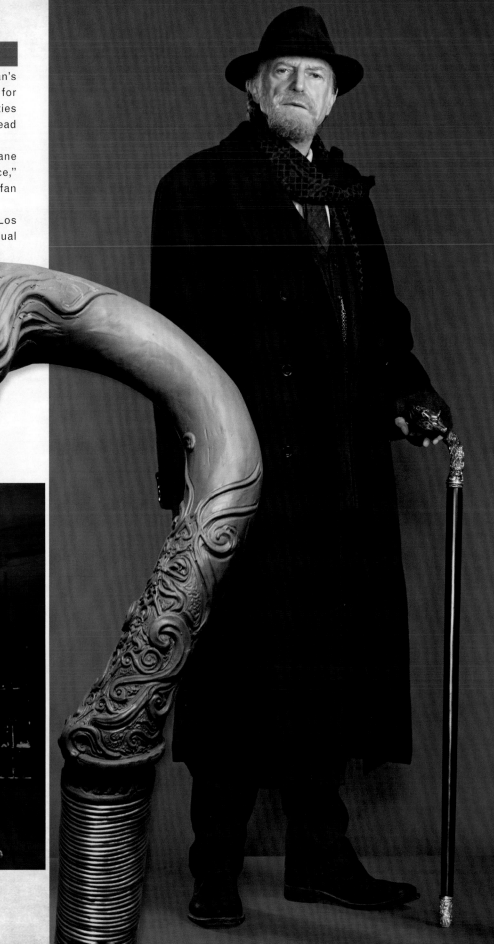

MIRIAM SETRAKIAN

One particular scene in the first episode of *The Strain* deftly communicates the eerie, melancholy history of Abraham Setrakian. Talking affectionately to his deceased wife's heart that he keeps in an airtight jar of cloudy liquid, Setrakian cuts his finger and lets the blood drip into the receptacle, the undead heart spasming with what appears to be delight.

In creating concept art depicting the heart, Guy Davis initially treated the organ like a wasp nest. "[I made it] brittle and dry, even though it was still fleshy," he says. "If you look at a wasp nest after part of it's been broken off, there's that papery layered feel that would look really grotesque for a human organ. Guillermo liked that, so we worked that up as an illustration."

The jar, meanwhile, needed an antique look, and props master Jim Murray began to feel that a store-bought jar wouldn't do: "It had to look old, have history, but also be large enough for visual effects elements."

The early assumption, based on the concept art, was that the jar would have to be made from scratch by a glass blower. However, on a tour of home decor stores, two possible jars were found. While customers browsed, Murray tested out the jars using a stand-in heart provided by the prosthetics team. "That was quite entertaining," he recalls. "It was hard to explain sometimes what we were doing."

Del Toro picked the jar he wanted, the lip was modified to hold a new lid and locking mechanism, and then the whole piece was aged to look hundreds of years old. The jar also satisfied the effects team, who needed a certain amount of space to add a digital, animated heart, layer in the digital blood, and include the vile bloodworms reaching up to feed as they detect Setrakian's offering.

OPPOSITE LEFT AND RIGHT Abraham Setrakian (David Bradley) with his signature cane.

OPPOSITE CENTER Concept sculpt of Setrakian's cane by Simon Lee.

ABOVE Strigoi heart in jar concept art by Guy Davis.

RIGHT The heart prop on set.

THE PAWNSHOP

A window into the cast-off trappings of a neighborhood's poor and the hideout of an aging warrior, Knickerbocker Loans and Curios in Spanish Harlem is one of the most important locations in the first season of *The Strain*. A store with a second-floor living space and a concealed basement armory, Abraham Setrakian's pawnshop needed to suggest hominess, a safe harbor of sorts, yet also reflect a man's iron will.

"It's provided a humble living for him," says actor David Bradley. "It's allowed him to keep his head below the surface all those years and not be noticed, while he plots his final destiny."

Working with early illustrations and key backgrounds from del Toro's team of concept artists, production designer Tamara Deverell sought a symmetrical, human space that showed that Setrakian was someone in control of his world, yet the location still had to exhibit the expressionistic flourishes you'd find in a graphic novel location. She imagined a place built in the 1800s and renovated in the 1930s, although she couldn't design it until an exterior was chosen somewhere in Toronto. Of two possibilities, del Toro picked a storefront with an entrance set back 11 feet from the sidewalk. The knickerbocker façade was built around it, including the hand-lettered shop sign and the three hanging, welded-metal spheres that have been a symbol of pawnbrokers for centuries. Next the windows were dressed with antiques and bric-a-brac. Deverell liked the depth the windows provided since it helped create the needed distance between the street and the interior for scenes that moved from outside to inside. Cameras on location could safely shoot facing the store without tipping off the audience that interiors were filmed elsewhere on an elaborately designed studio set.

OPPOSITE Exterior set for Abraham Setrakian's pawnshop hideaway.

TOP Concept art for the exterior of Setrakian's pawnshop by Francisco Ruiz Velasco.

ABOVE Setrakian (David Bradley) behind the counter of his shop.

RIGHT A production graphic used as reference for the pawnshop's many signs.

As for the pawnshop interior, the idea, says Deverell, "was to make it as rich and full as possible yet still make it a shootable space." Setrakian's loan desk, where he interacts with customers, was custom-built from oak, while Deverell used corroded tin tiles for the ceiling and existing windows and doors for a true period vibe. Authentic old counters and entire walls with shelving were put on wheels so they could be moved easily, but as shooting progressed, these moveable pieces often stayed put because they helped the actors believe they were in a small, lived-in environment.

Working from the color-coding that del Toro established early on, gold was chosen as the predominant hue for the set. "I wanted it to be the refuge of everything that was good," says del Toro. "I wanted it to feel like a sunset. Setrakian is the paladin of daylight, so we wanted a very warm type of golden."

Knowing del Toro's love of symbology, Deverell also added a secret pattern to the pawnshop's terrazzo floor that suggested a biohazard symbol. As for the secret panel door in the rear pawnshop wall that connects to the basement armory, Deverell took a brand new, expensive door system—the sliding kind found on vans—and gave it a patina of rust on the inside to suggest an aging mechanism.

As a way of visually connecting the pawnshop with the basement armory below, glass-block flooring was built into the pawnshop set. That way, when

action shifts to the underground armory, the glass block becomes a light source from above. (The two sets, however, were built next to each other on the soundstage.) Some intense scenic work was required to build the armory set, which is marked by foundation stone mixed with old brick, window wells, arches, and ornate iron trusswork inspired by a market building in Paris and flecked with blue. At one point, though, when the armory was being built, del Toro looked at a model of the final plan and said, "But where's the other staircase?" Although part of the set plan, Deverell had originally left it out because she wasn't clear about its purpose. Once the second back staircase was added, however, it

proved to be a striking addition and eventually came in handy for the vampire hunting team's escape later in the season.

"Guillermo is very hands-on with any set work and scenic work especially," says Deverell. "And he really does take time to talk to people on the crew. Everything doesn't just go through the production designer. If he's walking around the stage and the paint crew's there, he'll talk directly to them and say, 'Tell Tamara I love that. This is great.' It's just wonderful to work with a director and producer who's so in tune visually and so respectful to everybody."

Once Jim Murray's props team had decorated the set with dust-covered relics, arcane belongings, and the abandoned curios of desperate lives, the place started to take on a life of its own. For Bradley, stepping onto that set was like "finding the right shoes for the character. You feel just right. You're in that world. Just the design of the wallpaper and the furniture and the flat upstairs, as well as the objects in the shop, you think, 'I wouldn't change a thing.' It tells you an awful lot about the way a man has lived for all those years."

Invariably, the cast wandered around the pawnshop and armory sets so much in the first season that they all become covetous of the treasures on display. Corey Stoll admits having "a real problem with not touching stuff. I was just always picking up blades and playing with them. It was a boy's dream, that little hideaway."

OPPOSITE Drawing of the interior of Setrakian's pawn shop by Rustam Hasanov.
ABOVE LEFT Abraham Setrakian (David Bradley) behind the counter at his pawn shop.
BELOW Setrakian's downstairs lair, designed by Rustam Hasanov.

THESE PAGES Set photos showcase the interior of Abraham Setrakian's underground quarters, a hidden sanctum for plotting against The Master.

BIOHAZARD

AT THE BEGINNING OF *THE STRAIN*, the biggest problem in whip-smart CDC epidemiologist Ephraim Goodweather's life is the custody battle he faces with his wife Kelly over their son, Zack. That is, until a mysterious passenger jet filled with dead people upends his view of how bad—and terrifyingly unreal—a biological threat can get. When he's discredited and forced underground to fight for his family's life and the future of humanity, he must reevaluate everything.

Guillermo del Toro and Chuck Hogan created Eph to be, in some sense, the opposite of his last name. "I wanted him to be an irritatingly self-centered, fallible hero," says del Toro, "who is nevertheless the protagonist experiencing a full spiritual conversion."

Actor Corey Stoll, who plays Eph, lays out the hard road his character traverses during the early days of the epidemic: "He's always excelled at everything, and it all comes crashing down. Eph is not a believer in anything. It's all about proof and science, something that can be tested and replicated through experimentation. Nothing he's encountered before would [allow] him to believe vampires had existed. The first season serves to knock him down and convince him to try a different tack and accept his limitations."

In outfitting Eph, costume designer Luis Sequeira implemented the idea that bit-by-bit over the first season, his clothes would reflect a stripping away. "He starts the season all buttoned-up," says Sequeira. "Then throughout the season he loosens up. We take those layers off, down to one point where he's frazzled, and he takes off his button-down shirt, and he's in a T-shirt. We're breaking him down to being very casual."

In the second season, Eph has left academia and the casual look behind, and he and the hunters have become renegades with outfits to match. "We got them to the point where they're wearing scabbards, sheaths, and multiple weaponry, so they became warriors," says Sequeira. "It's still contemporary clothing, but he's gone from sports jacket, knit tie, and buttoned down shirt to fitted black military sweater, cargo pants, and boots."

Producer J. Miles Dale says that when you're making a show that deals explicitly with the supernatural, having an actor who has everyman acting chops grounds it in reality. "He's just a rock," says Dale. "To have a guy that good and naturalistic and believable in this elevated world, he keeps it real. He's kind of the key to the whole thing."

OPPOSITE Epidemiologist Ephraim Goodweather (Corey Stoll) is one of the story's flawed heroes.

ABOVE Eph in front of The Master's coffin.

LEFT Hazmat undersuit design concept art by Guy Davis.

BOTTOM RIGHT, CLOCKWISE FROM RIGHT Eph in happier times with wife, Kelly (Natalie Brown), and son, Zack (Ben Hyland); Eph and colleague Nora (Mia Maestro) in the lab; Eph taking aim at an old foe.

COUNTERCLOCKWISE FROM TOP LEFT Eph (Corey Stoll) and Nora (Mia Maestro) in the lab; Nora and her dementia-suffering mother, Mariela (Anne Betancourt); one-time lovers Nora (Maestro) and Eph (Stoll) in a tender embrace; a weaponized Nora ready to stop a strigoi attack.

OPPOSITE Nora Martinez, blade in hand, in the New York subway.

NORA MARTINEZ

DR. NORA MARTINEZ is a biochemist with a social medicine background, but she cares more about people than the diseases that threaten them. She is the type of strong, brilliant scientist you'd want on your team—and that's exactly what Eph thought when he first met her and asked her to join him at the CDC. She became a trusted colleague and Eph's sometime lover during their years of working together. But the devastating rapidity of this disturbing new virus forces the humanist in Nora to confront some uncomfortable truths about their relationship and her own view of humanity, especially when her own mother succumbs.

"She's going to find strength in places she never thought she would," says Mia Maestro, who plays Nora. "She's gone through a lot and is a wonderful biochemist whose job probably takes over her life. She thinks there has to be a cure. She has a different methodology for how to deal with things, and I think it comes from heart and a female perspective. Of course there's doubt, but I love that about Nora. There are a lot of gray [areas]."

The Nora of the books was Mexican, but following Maestro's casting, she was made Argentine to match the actress's own heritage. There was another key change, too: "Guillermo del Toro and Carlton Cuse rewrote Nora for me to be a lot more active than in the books. In the books, she stays home while the men fight. But that's not the Nora of the TV show. And yeah, I like the fighting."

DEATH FROM ABOVE

The first large-scale set seen in *The Strain* is Regis Air flight 753, a 777 holding hundreds of passengers, each unsuspecting of the evil that lurks below them in the storage hold. When the plane lands at JFK and is revealed to essentially be a parked cemetery sitting on the tarmac, Eph and Nora venture on board to examine what could have wiped out the vast majority of the plane's human cargo.

Destined to appear only in the pilot, the Regis airplane set proved to be one of the more demanding to assemble. The sixty-foot-long interior was really two different sets connected together. The cockpit and business class were borrowed from the movie *Non-Stop* and shipped from New York to Toronto. The coach section and flight attendant area in back, meanwhile, came from a rental place in Los Angeles. "These guys actually take planes, cut them up, make film sets out of them, and rent the pieces," says production designer Tamara Deverell. Deverell and her crew then went to work painting and reupholstering the two sections of the set so they would look distinct and also meet Guillermo del Toro's color palette directions regarding the play between amber tones and blue hues: "We tested colors and went for a very distinct blue/gray tone throughout the plane."

As for shooting at an airport, the production came into some luck when Toronto's Pearson International Airport let *The Strain* film at their closed Terminal 1, which is normally used for staff training. Even better, says Deverell, "the inside terminal conformed to our color code: It was all blue-grays, these completely monochromatically cool tones. When I saw it, I thought, 'Wow.' If we'd had all the money in the world, we'd have built it that way." On the tarmac, meanwhile, the production's lights had to be tilted toward the shooting area so as not to face nearby runways and endanger incoming traffic.

Eph and Nora's special hazmat suits—a skintight layer beneath loose biohazard outerwear—were initially designed in the concept stage by Guy Davis, then custom-made by a company that specializes in containment suits. Dozens of breathing and mask systems were tested before del Toro approved of the apparatus props master Jim Murray eventually built. The helmet system, meanwhile, with its glowing yellow interior and microphone set-up, was a collaboration across many departments, including lighting, sound, wardrobe, and props.

BIOHAZARD SEALED

753

TOP LEFT CDC colleagues Eph (Corey Stoll) and Nora (Mia Maestro) in hazmat suits, ready to investigate the plane.

RIGHT Rendered illustration of the Regis Air bodies by Tamara Deverell.

OPPOSITE LEFT Luggage tag designed by Jason Graham.

OPPOSITE RIGHT The dead from Regis Air flight 753 sealed in bags at the airport.

NEW YORK CITY PEST CONTROL

EXTERMINATION
OFFICER

FET
VASILIY

EXPIRES 2030 SEPT 04

PEST CONTROL
OFFICER

BPC

CITY OF
NEW YORK

VASILIY FET

AS HIDDEN IN PLAIN SIGHT as a big, broad-shouldered Ukrainian can be, before the outbreak, solitary exterminator Vasiliy Fet patrolled the sewers beneath the city on the hunt for vermin. It's that knowledge and curiosity about how subterranean life operates that gives him a special leg-up when the target of his eradication method shifts from rats to vampires. "He's thriving in a world that's falling," says Kevin Durand, who plays Fet. "Vasiliy's not a punch-your-card kind of guy about his job. This was a specific choice for him, and he decided he would be the absolute best at what he does."

During the writing of the first book, Chuck Hogan felt that the story was calling out for a counterpoint to Eph's medical-minded approach, so he created Fet, for whom saving lives is all about killing. Guillermo del Toro instantly fell in love with this unlikely vanquisher. "He's one of the greatest

characters in the trilogy," says del Toro. "I had so much fun writing him that he derailed the structure of the second and third books as he became more and more heroic."

Del Toro was also quick to okay Durand playing Fet when executive producer Carlton Cuse introduced the actor to him. "I'd worked with Kevin on *Lost*," says Cuse. "He played a super badass mercenary. But as I got to know Kevin, I knew there was this whole other side to the guy—sweet and smart—so when I read Fet, I pictured Kevin Durand in my brain."

Fet also forms a swift, almost father-son-like bond with Abraham Setrakian based on a shared understanding of the importance of being unsentimental about killing when a job has to be done. "They're both men of action," says Durand. "That's why they immediately understand each other."

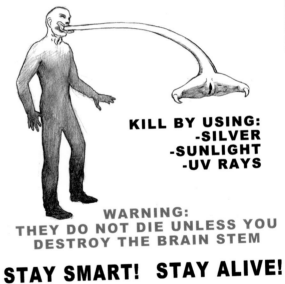

OPPOSITE TOP, TOP LEFT, AND TOP RIGHT Pest control warrior Vasiliy Fet (Kevin Durand) has a mercenary approach to vampire hunting.

OPPOSITE BOTTOM Set photos show Fet's bachelor pad.

MIDDLE AND BOTTOM RIGHT Pest control badge design and Wilson's logo design by Jason Graham.

ABOVE Beware sign designed by Juan Pablo Garcia Tames.

TUNNEL OF BLOOD

The Strain is true to Guillermo del Toro's obsessions in many ways, and this is particularly apparent when it goes underground to the dark network of New York City subway tunnels where Vasiliy Fet plies his trade as an exterminator and where The Master's unholy brood nests. For del Toro, it's what lies beneath that often represents the scariest threat—from the subway-inspired *Mimic* and the sewer-based action scenes of *Blade II* through the underworld-set *Hellboy* and the depths from which the monsters in *Pacific Rim* emanate.

Tunnels, therefore, would prove instrumental to the arc of the first season, used as they are for scenes of exploration, discovery, and confrontation between our heroes and the strigoi. Although Toronto has a closed subway area that film crews often utilize (it was used in some scenes for *The Strain*), it wouldn't be adequate for a show that featured numerous underground sequences throughout the breadth of a whole season. What production designer Tamara Deverell needed was a set they could dress and re-dress at will, and to that end, a "Franken-tunnel" set was built out of scavenged tunnel sets from three different productions: the movies *Pompeii* and *Mortal Instruments: City of Bones* and the TV show *Beauty and the Beast*.

ABOVE AND RIGHT Different sections of *The Strain*'s tunnel set.

FAR RIGHT Illustration of The Master in the tunnels by Juan Pablo Garcia Tames.

OPPOSITE The Master's coffin prop in the tunnel set.

Cobbled together in the series' warehouse studio in the east end of Toronto, it became the multipurpose tunnel set—almost 200 feet long and 35 feet tall at its highest point—for any number of underground scenes. The scenic crew stayed busy as they transformed the set to become everything from The Master's lair circa World War II to a modern-day empty stretch of subway (with crew-built tracks) to The Master's modern-day lair where Fet, Eph, and the team encounter a vast nest of sleeping vampires. "The crew was constantly remaking it to look like stone, then like brick, then older brick, then newer brick," says Deverell. "There's a lot of great dressing, too, with endless pipes and electrical panels."

Having originally worked with del Toro on *Mimic*, which drew from the mythology surrounding New York City's subterranean transportation aesthetic, Deverell understood the need to make sure this aspect of *The Strain* met his needs. "We really worked hard to bring what you might think exists below the streets of New York into the show."

DUTCH VELDERS

MERCURIAL, TALENTED, AND EDGY, hacker Dutch Velders is a new character created for the TV show by Carlton Cuse and Chuck Hogan, who wanted to bring more diverse female characters into the show's universe. Introduced as the Eldritch Palmer hiree responsible for shutting down the Internet, Dutch takes stock of the horrific consequences of her actions and joins the vampire hunters' cause. It's a fraught match-up at first: To them, she's one of the reasons the plague exists, and her default attitude is feistiness. Ultimately, however, the group begin to realize that Dutch is trying to make things right.

"She's a loner who doesn't want to be a loner," says Ruta Gedmintas, who plays Dutch. "She's built up this tough skin, but she still wants people to like her. As a hacker, she's never really had to think about anybody but herself, but now she's starting to realize she can't act that way

anymore." Helping that transition is the growing bond with Fet and the realization that they both have much in common. "It starts to open her up a little, seeing that other people feel like they're on the outside."

Dressing Dutch was a matter of matching her eccentric vibe and contrasting the other hunters' seriousness. "We wanted to shake it up," says costume designer Luis Sequeira. "She wore stripes, amber-patterned pants and high-lace boots, and a suede and faux-fur long vest. She's quite eclectic, as opposed to being reserved like everyone else."

OPPOSITE Ace hacker Dutch Velders (Ruta Gedmintas) with friend Nikki (Nicola Correia Damude) during the convenience store siege.

TOP LEFT Poster created by the production department for Dutch's apartment.

TOP RIGHT Dutch takes aim.

MIDDLE LEFT Dutch is taken into custody.

BOTTOM LEFT AND RIGHT Dutch's tattoo design by Rabab Ali.

GUS ELIZALDE

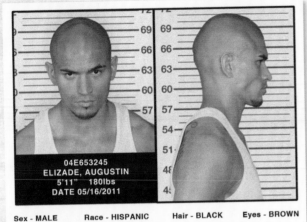

04E653245
ELIZADE, AUGUSTIN
5'11" 180lbs
DATE 05/16/2011

Sex - MALE   Race - HISPANIC   Hair - BLACK   Eyes - BROWN

DOB - 05/08/1992   SID# - 8452125421E   CARD# -00065325

A PRODUCT OF THE STREETS, Mexican gangbanger Augustin "Gus" Elizalde starts out as a freelance employee of The Master, driving the vampire's coffin into Manhattan. When the contagion starts, however, Gus eventually realizes which side he needs to be on and becomes the fiercest of hunters, even joining forces with vampires dedicated to wiping out the worst of their own kind.

"He's got a good heart," says Miguel Gomez, who plays Gus. "He goes through some pretty rough stuff, but it's going to make him the best possible warrior. The sickness hit home for him literally, and the fact that he had a part in spreading it . . . he wants to make up for it, for his mother,

his brother, and his best friend. Losing people will change you."

Gomez was especially excited to explore someone who wasn't just a stereotypical gangster. "*The Strain* shows why a person comes to be like this," he says. "It's really protection. It's his armor for the war he faces every day [on the streets]. Fighting these creatures is not new to him. He already knows that he can step outside every day and possibly die. So he's equipped to handle this war."

COUNTERCLOCKWISE FROM TOP LEFT
Gus's mug shot created by the art department; Gus (Miguel Gomez) armed and ready to take on the strigoi; Gus with Sun Hunter Vaun (Stephen McHattie); Gus at the Tandoori Palace restaurant.

OPPOSITE Gangbanger turned vampire hunter Gus Elizalde (Gomez).

A MASTER PLAN

THE ALLIANCE OF ancient evil and modern greed that forms the dark engine of *The Strain* is malignly majestic in its scope. For a dormant curse to become a lasting regime of supremacy, a handful of opportunistic individuals must come together and use powers human and inhuman to see the plan through. One player is the kingpin of this otherworldly scourge, two others are his on-the-ground soldiers, and the last is a pawn. Together they're a force to be reckoned with, the front line in a malicious battle to remake the planet.

THE MASTER

CENTURIES-OLD, EVER-HUNGRY, DEVIOUS, deadly, and the leader of an army of vampires he can control with his mind, The Master is the driving force behind the plan for worldwide domination that puts *The Strain* in motion. Although the story of giant-sized Albanian nobleman Jusef Sardu and his mysterious transformation is told as a gruesome fairy tale of sorts early on in the first del Toro/Hogan novel, it was decided that for season one of *The Strain* The Master should remain a purely scary, lethal entity of unexplained provenance.

"I knew The Master was going to be more threatening when he was a shadow and a figure," says Guillermo del Toro, who, in devising his story's key villain, wasn't interested in the typical emaciated vampire. "I thought it would be nice to make him bigger and more muscular with bigger bones."

PREVIOUS PAGES Concept art for the top panel engraving of The Master's coffin by Guy Davis.

LEFT Cloak design for The Master by Keith Thompson.

ABOVE Jusef Sardu design, drawing by Keith Thompson.

OPPOSITE Concept art for The Master's eyes by Keith Thompson.

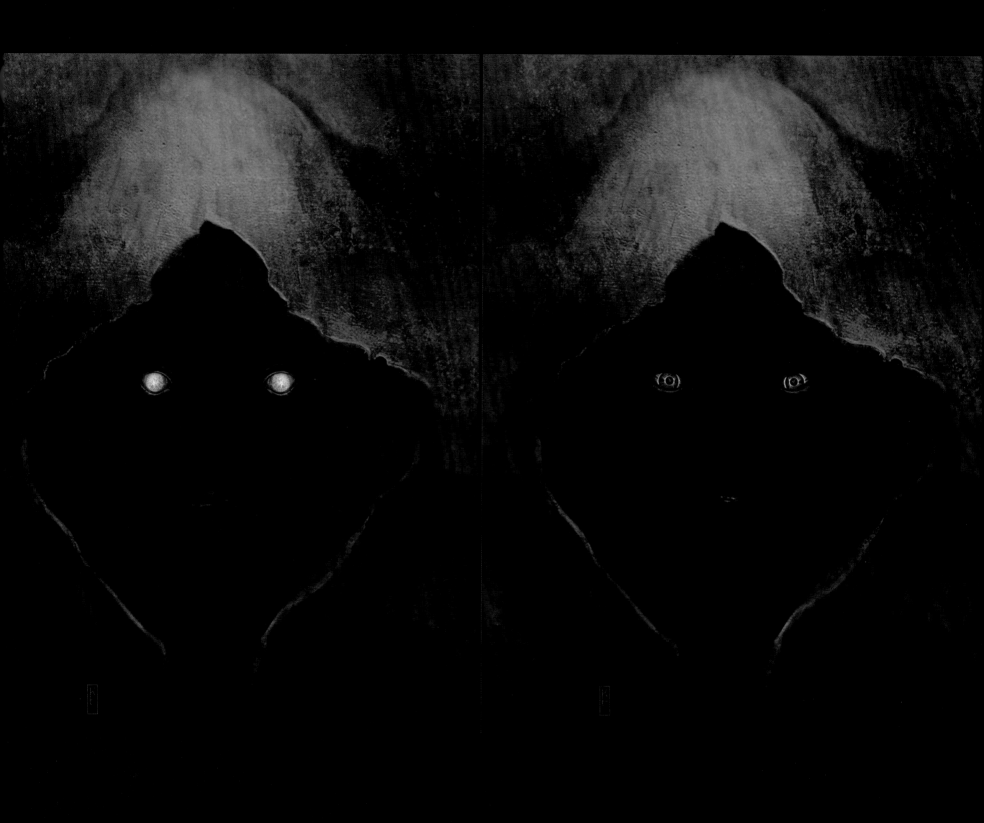

THESE AND FOLLOWING PAGES Concept art for The Master's cloak and costume design, drawings by Keith Thompson.

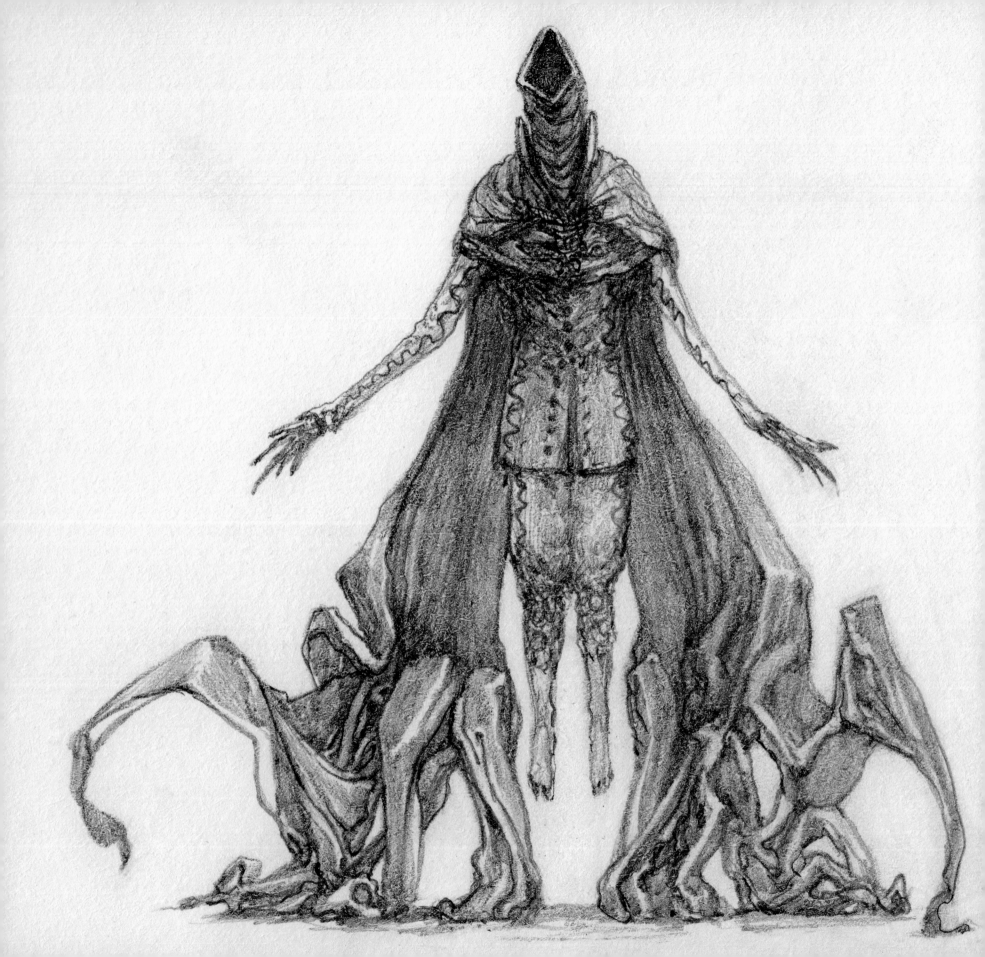

Early concept art for Sardu/The Master reflects this, depicting a hulking man of breadth made even more imposing by heavy hunting robes. Much of the art also shows a mouth that massively dislocates to reveal a fully pronounced stinger. Says del Toro, "The Master and the older vampires develop an enhanced mouth, so they have these curves at the end that allow their mouths to disengage wider and propel the stinger faster."

The pilot originally called for more prominent visuals of The Master, specifically shots of him using his stinger in an attack, so creature shop artists Sean Sansom and Steve Newburn made a full animatronic upper torso of the character with a mechanical stinger. With heavy daily input from del Toro, the pair worked from small prototype concept statues built by Simon Lee during the concept art process, as well as a larger makeup sculpture created by Mario Torres. "You could see the jaw dislocating and the mouth opening two or three times wider than it should," says Sean Sansom of the puppet.

"Guillermo also wanted the eyes to bug out when they were feeding, then roll back."

When the decision was made to not show The Master's face at all in the pilot in favor of a few fleeting glimpses of a cloaked, darting figure, the head/torso puppet was scrapped, never to be used again. The thinking was that using such a mechanism would require too much post-production work and expense. Nevertheless, prosthetics for actor Robert Maillet, the 6'11" French-Canadian wrestler-turned-actor cast as The Master, still had to be made for his eventual reveal.

The creature team first made a lifecast of Maillet, after which the prosthetics were broken up into eleven separate appliances, including the back of the head, top of the head, forehead, face, teeth, hands, bulbous wattles, and the pointed ears—all of which had to be blended to look seamless. As for the ears, del Toro wanted them translucent, so they were made from a different material that allowed light to show through the skin. The wattles were meticulously painted and glued on to the neck. The eyes were intended to suggest an eclipsed sun, an idea del Toro thought "would be kind of cute and horrible at the same time."

TOP LEFT Animatronic version of The Master.

LEFT Conceptual sculpt of The Master by Simon Lee.

TOP RIGHT Sculpture artist Mario Torres Jr. putting the finishing touches on the animatronic Master.

As for The Master's hands, which have been likened to sausage fingers, Steve Newburn says that with the exception of the extended middle finger, the prosthetic is only an eighth of an inch thick. In other words, Maillet's hands really are that big. "When Robert's stunt double came in for the season finale, the makeup fit him fine, but when I put the gloves on him, they were so baggy he could stick both hands into one of Robert's gloves," says Newburn. "And this was a big guy, too! Ultimately I put heavy wool gloves on the stunt guy, then stuffed his hands in there, and you still could have fit my hand in there too."

TOP RIGHT Guillermo del Toro checking how light hits The Master (Robert Maillet) in full makeup.

ABOVE Applying The Master prosthetics on to Maillet.

LEFT Maillet wearing the fully applied prosthetics for The Master.

RIGHT Sculpt of The Master's left hand with its extended finger.

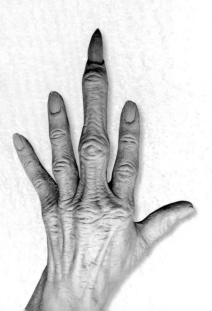

All in all, getting Maillet into his Master prosthetic was at first a four-hour process that, by the end of the first season, had been efficiently whittled down to two and a half hours.

And that was still before the wardrobe department dressed him for the shoot. The Master's sartorial look, on one level, was simple: He'd be clad in the same substantial nobleman's robes he wore the night he was turned. But on another level, this "monolithic" look, as costume designer Luis Sequeira calls it, was not nearly so simple. Says del Toro, "I thought he would accumulate hundreds of years' worth of patching from repairing those robes. As some fall away, he puts on a new one until he's like a living mound of rags."

Because of Maillet's size and the amount of fabric it would take to dress him, Sequeira designed initially in half-scale, then moved to full scale when he was happy with all the texturing and details. "I wanted to give the cameraman the ability to shoot it at any angle, so the audience would always have something interesting to look at," says Sequeira, who included fine touches such as brass wolfs'-head buttons on the frock coat and copper embroidery created in India. In all, 250 meters of fabric were purchased, from rayon wool and hopsack to silk and linens, all just to make The Master's seven-layered, double-lining cape.

Even after outfitting Maillet, Sequeira determined the shoulders weren't wide enough, so padding was added to create more breadth plus humps that suggested a tucked-in wing. The boots, meanwhile, had to be custom-made, since Maillet wears a size-22 shoe. His footwear was also adapted into platform boots, taking the towering actor over the 7-foot mark. Finally, adding aging and distressing effects to the cloak material created the sense of time's passage. In total, one "hero" cloak—the enormous one Maillet would wear—and four stunt cloaks were created for the first season. Fans would get an even better look at it in the second season, however, when the long-awaited origins of The Master were dramatized. "[We made it] again," says Sequeira, "but not broken down. [It's] fully fashioned in its entirety, with a lighter color palette of all the same fabrics. Basically, it's the pre-dirty version."

LEFT A lighting test for The Master (Robert Maillet).

OPPOSITE TOP LEFT The design of The Master would be altered to remove the character's nose.

OPPOSITE TOP RIGHT The cloaked Master in his underground lair.

OPPOSITE BOTTOM A made-up Maillet with actor Sean Astin (Jim Kent).

Everyone on *The Strain* knew how much Maillet had to go through before cameras could roll on his scenes, especially the similarly imposing Kevin Durand (just five inches shorter than Maillet). "Because of our size, we've spent a good portion of our careers wearing all kinds of insane prosthetics to transform us," says Durand. "The last thing he needs is me commenting on it, like, 'Dude, you must be hot in there, huh?' But he's such a sweet guy and doing a great job. He's the only fella I've ever worked with where I walk by him and kind of straighten up my spine so as not to feel too emasculated by his physical prowess!"

It's not always Maillet onscreen as the Jusef Sardu incarnation of The Master, though. For some movement scenes, it's choreographer Roberto Campanella in one of the stunt cloaks, and in a few special instances—such as The Master's skittering away after killing Bishop in the pilot or escaping off the edge of the building in the season one finale—he's a product of the digital effects team.

"Guillermo had a very specific reference that he drew on a piece of paper for us," says visual effects supervisor Dennis Berardi. "It's a sort of spider walk, but he wanted the tentacles of his cloak to flair and make this really interesting star pattern with flourishes. He didn't want him to fly. He wanted him to move across the ground quickly."

Getting the movement right using performance-based animation is an iterative process, says Berardi. It starts with scanning Robert Maillet in full make-up to create a digital double, then putting that digital double to work in the computer. "We just do take after take after take, like you would with an actor on a set," says Berardi. "We'll show Guillermo a blocking pass, then we tweak, then show him a take, then tweak again. Sometimes it's ten or twelve takes until we get a performance that works for the edit and starts to be believable and fun." Without that back-and-forth, refining, and tweaking, says Berardi, the work doesn't breathe, "and you can get really bad CGI."

Coffin Latch

Coffin Latch
-1 -Outside-

THE COFFIN

The Master's mode of intercontinental transportation may have technically been a Boeing 777, but what concealed his stowaway status was the enormous coffin he resided in for the journey. It's the kind of black box no one would want to find.

During the concept art stage, Guy Davis was tasked with the design and graphics for this essential object in the story's mythology. Although the coffin had already been rendered in the comic books, del Toro told Davis he could chart his own path, as long as it was ornately carved, ancient-looking, and demonstrably creepy. He envisioned a monolith of sorts that could act as an iconic standing cabinet towering above onlookers rather than lying on the ground beneath the eye-level of humans. Inspired by medieval artwork, specifically the *danse macabre* genre that reveled in images of death as a way of reminding a fragile humanity of its ultimate destination, Davis took a storytelling approach to the surface design.

"The top had a heaven motif, the bottom had a hell motif, the sides were man and woman," says Davis. "The front of the coffin focused on the coming eclipse, with death blocking out the sun and the skeletal dead being born from the fallen bodies and rising to meet the eclipsing grim reaper en masse. I just filled up all

OPPOSITE TOP Keyframe art by Francisco Ruiz Velasco of Eph and Nora examining the coffin.

OPPOSITE BOTTOM Coffin latches designed by Bartol Rendulic.

THIS PAGE Designs for The Master's intricate coffin by Guy Davis.

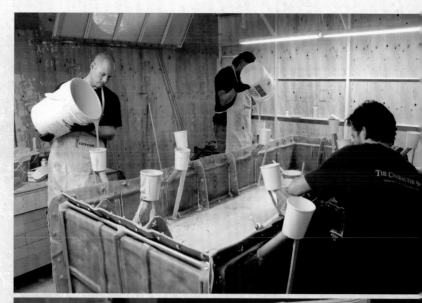

sides with death." Only the back was left blank, since in the story it's built by the young Abraham Setrakian, who believes it's to be used as a standing cabinet, destined to stand up against a wall with its back section covered.

Once del Toro approved of the labyrinthine designs, creature artists Sean Sansom and Steve Newburn printed them out full size and began sculpting the sides from large panels of clay. It took Sansom, Newburn, and two other workers two entire months to hand-carve and sculpt every panel, which is one reason Sansom and Newburn considered the coffin to be their single biggest project for season one of the show. From the sculpts, molds were made, then carpenters constructed the coffin out of lightweight fiberglass, while scenic artists put on the finishing touches. When, later in the season, del Toro needed the coffin to be manipulated onscreen in a way that indicated genuine heaviness, the fiberglass was cut apart, and special effects coordinator Warren Appleby's crew added a full steel skeleton that made the prop weigh over 1,500 pounds. And for the flash-back that required the young Abraham Setrakian to smash part of it, the bottom panel was replaced by carved wood to get the proper splintering effect.

In the end, The Master's coffin counted as a significant early step forward in establishing one of the show's signature artistic elements. "It was such a beau-tiful piece," says Appleby of the coffin. "It photographed so well. To stand there and see that all this was actually hand-carved by Steve's crew . . . it was spectac-ular work."

THOMAS EICHHORST

SINISTER, EERILY CALM, with a grin that cuts like a knife, eminent strigoi Thomas Eichhorst is no stranger to following orders, since he spent his pre-transformation days as a high-ranking SS officer during World War II. It was in this role that he met the young Abraham Setrakian while stationed at a concentration camp. Brought to life by German actor Richard Sammel, the devilishly entertaining Eichhorst quickly became the series' most compelling love-to-hate character.

"As a showrunner, when I find an actor I really enjoy writing for, then I'll write more and more stuff for him or her," says executive producer Carlton Cuse. "And in the case of Richard, he was so engaging that we wrote more for him than we originally planned. All the writers loved him."

Sammel says Eichhorst is a man corrupted by an extreme Darwinistic ideology, first espoused by the Nazis and then The Master. "If Hitler promised a thousand-year Reich, then The Master is fulfilling it," says Sammel. "It's a very strong belief in the promise of eternal life. It was huge for me that this guy decides to become a vampire, because it was either that or suicide."

When it came to performing the role, Sammel developed the idea that Eichhorst should move as little as possible to accentuate his overall physical oddness: "I got rid of all the little nods, movements, and indirect bodily speaking that humans use, because when you eliminate all that, it's weird. Is he listening? Not listening? Does he agree with you? I trusted in less energy and found that what works is being simple and direct. I also got that from nature, studying a lot of animals. How a cat walks or a snake moves."

In dressing Eichhorst, costume designer Luis Sequeira pored over many suits looking for something streamlined and nondescript. "One of Guillermo's things is making sure everything's very well-tailored," says Sequeira. "So we found this beautiful suit—very au courant but still classic—and then mocked up the same suit for stunt sequences. For the shirt, we went with a puce, which on camera didn't look like anything, very odd-looking and slightly off. White would make him pop, and we wanted him to blend away, so he could just slip into a crowd."

The well-tailored look was briefly abandoned though for Eichhorst's season two flashback, which revealed his pre-Nazi life as a run-of-the-mill salesman. Sequeira delighted in stripping away Eichhorst's exquisite wardrobe and replacing it with something far less urbane: "I wanted to make him a little sloppy. He was not at the top of his game. So we gave him an ill-fitting suit, a tie, and a sweater. It was fun making him look younger and not refined."

Sammel believes that Eichhorst's impeccable attire—which includes "wearing" a human face—is more than just a guise to blend in. It's the one link to humanity he cultivates. "It's his narcissism," says Sammel. "I think he still is a little bit human, and it's a weakness. As in, let's keep what humanity has produced the best of: nice clothes, classical music, elegance, being distinguished. I even pretend he prefers eating to sucking the blood from people."

HALT! STOJ!

ACHTUNG!
GEFAHRENZONE

OPPOSITE Exquisitely tailored Thomas Eichhorst (Richard Sammel) is The Master's right-hand vamp.

TOP RIGHT Eichhorst proves that not all vampires are afraid of crucifixes.

RIGHT Eichhorst, during his time as a Nazi in World War II, admires the young Abraham Setrakian's coffin work.

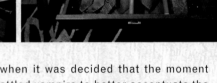

THE FACE OF EVIL

One of the most disturbing scenes in the entire first season of *The Strain* sees Eichhorst affixing his human visage, a creepily satirical take on the classic morning routine of "putting your face on" at the vanity table. The opening scene of episode three, this show-stopping sequence was a last-minute addition del Toro made to the shooting schedule. "I thought it would be a great scene," he says. "I always wanted to have fun with that."

Del Toro had mentioned the idea in passing to the creature shop crew, who agreed it'd be an effective set-up, but because it wasn't in early drafts of the script—the ones provided months before so the physical effects teams could have plenty of time to prepare—they put it out of their mind. When it suddenly showed up on the schedule for the episode three shoot, then moved up even sooner, it meant making Eichhorst's various face applications—including ears and neck—in a hurry. Then, a nose request came in at 2 a.m. the night before the sequence was to be shot. (Until this scene was invented and filmed, the plan had been that only The Master would be shown noseless.)

Meanwhile, the production design crew, also working under a time crunch, had quickly cobbled together art deco pieces and ready-to-assemble furniture, putting them together in the tasteful but darkly lit lobby of a condo building, the location that would briefly become Eichhorst's private quarters. (For season two, a more permanent set was built for scenes of Eichhorst's home.) With the prosthetic nose complete and ready to be used in the sequence, Sammel's actual nose was painted green on set, so the visual effects team could later replace it digitally with a hollowed-out socket. After the scene was filmed, del Toro directed additional second-unit shots when it was decided that the moment needed a closer look at the noseless, wattled vampire to better accentuate the transformation.

Notably, the scene is also a winking nod to the venerable art of prosthetics, only in the opposite vein: turning a monster into a human. Creature effects supervisor Steve Newburn jokes, "From a real-world standpoint, that's hours and hours of makeup, and yet he sits there and does it in two minutes on camera! And we always wondered, 'Where does he get his pieces from?'"

Sounds like The Master may have friends in the film industry . . .

TOP LEFT Eichhorst (Richard Sammel) at his vanity table prior to applying his "human" face.

TOP RIGHT Sammel shooting Eichhorst's prosthetics scene.

ABOVE Furniture and prop pieces for the Eichhorst scene.

OPPOSITE LEFT A mold of Richard Sammel's head as the noseless Eichhorst.

OPPOSITE TOP RIGHT Sammel in Eichhorst's strigoi makeup.

OPPOSITE BOTTOM RIGHT Sammel with a green nose that will be removed in post-production and replaced with an exposed cavity through the use of digital effects.

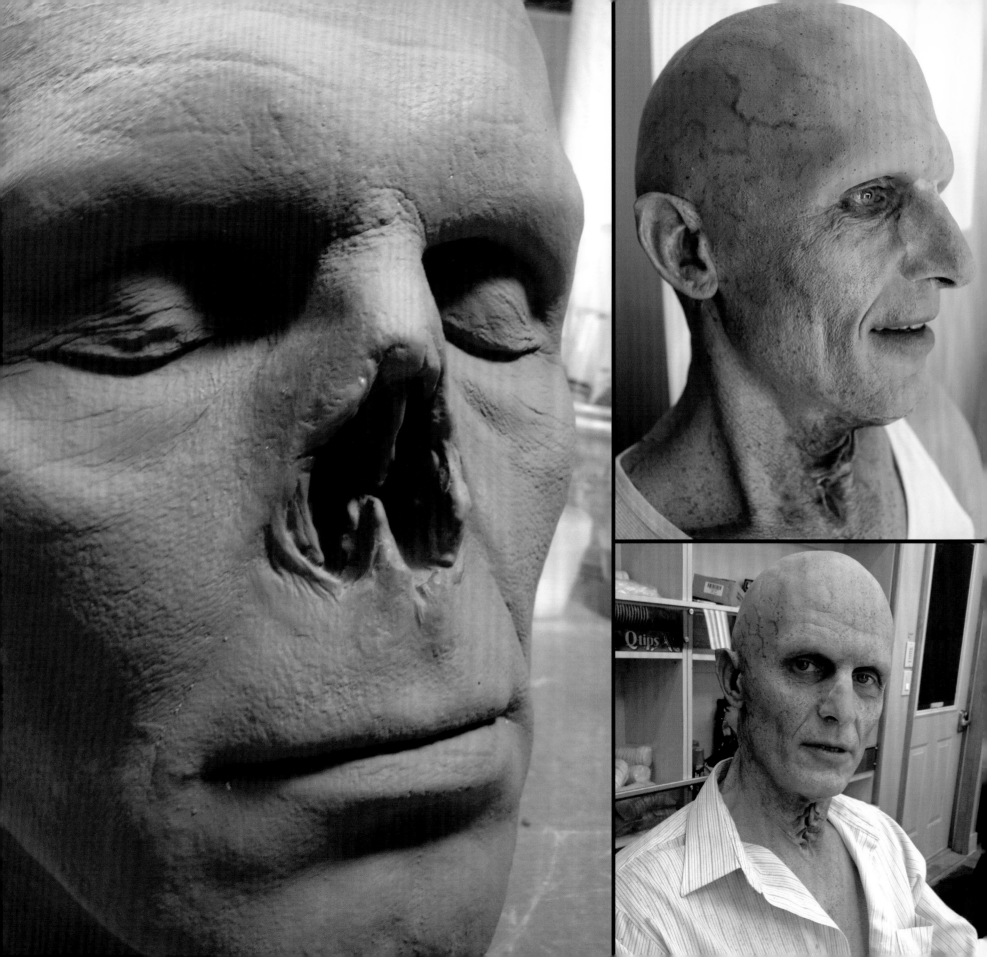

CONCENTRATION CAMP SET

Some of Eichhorst's most dramatic scenes are the flashbacks that take place at a Third Reich extermination camp, the location where Eichhorst first encounters young prisoner Abraham Setrakian. For production designer Tamara Deverell, the challenge of coming up with this set was creating the sense of a concentration camp without making it too real. "It's too fresh in the history of humanity," says Deverell. "So you want almost a graphic-novel sense of what a concentration camp would be."

One of Toronto's oldest sewage treatment plants, which held many old brick buildings and had a smokestack, stood in for the exterior of the camp. The prisoner barracks interior was built on the soundstage, with bunk beds constructed by the crew. To reconfigure the same space into the camp's woodworking shop— where young Setrakian builds The Master's coffin—the beds were removed and built-in walls added. "It was a way to put more into the build and get more bang for your buck by using those two places," says Deverell.

As for the train shown in the flashbacks, the art department and visual effects worked in tandem. Deverell's team built a boxcar and transported it to the sewage plant location along with rail tracks, while visual effects supervisor Dennis Berardi and his team at the VFX house Mr. X Inc. replicated it and used digital effects to create a train pulling dozens of cars.

OPPOSITE TOP LEFT Computer rendering of boxcar set by Matthew Morgan.

OPPOSITE BOTTOM LEFT Photo of the final concentration camp prisoner sleeping quarters set.

OPPOSITE RIGHT Concept art of The Master prowling the concentration camp by Keith Thompson.

ABOVE The concentration camp woodshop set.

RIGHT A series of images shows how a computer-generated train was added to the concentration camp set.

ELDRITCH PALMER

NAMED AFTER AN OPPORTUNISTIC TYCOON in a story by legendary sci-fi writer Philip K. Dick, industrialist Eldritch Palmer is one of the world's wealthiest and most powerful men. However, with his health failing, Palmer is willing to risk everything in a bid for the one thing he doesn't have: immortality. Having staved off death through a series of organ transplants, he fully intends to submit to The Master's vile version of longevity. As Palmer uses his money and influence to pull the levers that put The Master's plan into motion—controlling politicians, purposefully mismanaging the response to the plague, shutting down the Internet—the clock is ticking on his own corporeal obsolescence, unless his pact with the strigoi leader can yield his biggest acquisition yet.

In the books, Palmer is primarily a cocooned string-puller in the Stoneheart Group penthouse but became a more active Machiavellian-type character in the series. "We really embellished and expanded the plan by which New York fell and the fact that Palmer was this super-rich guy who was The Master's human helper," says executive producer Carlton Cuse. "He's intimately involved in crafting a whole set of chess moves that are going to bring New York down."

Jonathan Hyde, the British actor who plays Palmer, likens his character's outlook to the way Stalin relished his role as Russia's dictator: "Stalin could play any number of games in order to get what he wanted, and it was the game-playing he enjoyed almost more than anything. I wouldn't put Palmer too far from that club. He's an unlovable monster in many ways."

TOP Eldritch Palmer (Jonathan Hyde) is the financial muscle behind The Master's operation.

ABOVE Illustration of Palmer's apartment by Bartol Rendulic.

OPPOSITE Concept art of Palmer's apartment by Keith Thompson.

PALMER

AERIE

STONEHEART GROUP SET

For Palmer's skyscraper fortress in the Stoneheart building to be effective, it needed to be a space that emanated chilly power, while reflecting the mind of a megalomaniac in cahoots with an ancient vampire. Concept drawings suggested an enormous, Frank Lloyd Wright–inspired space, and with budgetary concerns in mind, production designer Tamara Deverell made judicious choices to realize this

key interior. She kept the set tall, used real marble on the floor for an unmistakably rich touch, but instead of using green screen and visual effects for the views outside the massive windows, she allocated the funds to a heavily Photoshopped backdrop photograph of the New York skyline that did the job just as well.

Deverell takes her cues from character as often as possible, so to express Palmer's off-putting alliance with the vampire world, she designed a deliberately asymmetrical set. "It forced certain camera angles, and everything felt shifted and off-kilter," says Deverell. "And that's Palmer's world."

As for the corporate logo that dominates the fireplace—a mythic-looking, hammer-wielding figure—Deverell and del Toro discussed Stoneheart's various interests, including nuclear power and electrical energy, and created symbols that suggested 1930s-style Soviet sculpture iconography mixed with the kind of raised carvings seen in Art Deco buildings. Using concept drawings by artists

Guy Davis and Toronto-based illustrator Bartol Rendulic for reference, a sculptor hand-carved the Stoneheart logo out of Styrofoam, then Deverell's crew of scenic artists gave it a stone-like finish. "I thought there'd be a Francis Bacon or some masterpiece of value," jokes Jonathan Hyde about his character's art choices. "Instead I've got this gruesome piece of quasi-fascist bas-relief!"

The gruesomeness didn't end there, either. Although a few Roman and Greek sculptures adorn the mostly spare space, the question preoccupying the production design department was: What should go on the shelves? In an especially unpleasant decorative touch, del Toro suggested organs in jars:

STONEHEART
GROUP INC.

the displayed leftovers of dozens of Palmer's death-dodging transplants. "It's typically insane but absolutely perfect," says Deverell. "The set decorator and I, our mouths fell open. We looked at each other and laughed. We actually had to order fake organs. We talked about getting pig organs from a slaughterhouse, but you couldn't do that to the crew—the smell and some poor guy having to change them."

Again, Hyde was floored by what he had to look at on set: "I guess Eldritch might take certain satisfaction from thinking, 'Was that [organ] from Guatemala? Who were these people whose sides were ripped open in order to keep me alive?'"

GABRIEL BOLIVAR

ONE OF FOUR SURVIVORS from the incident on Regis Air flight 753, Gabriel Bolivar is an already vampiric-looking rock musician as season one begins, with a legion of devoted fans. Self-involved, image-conscious, and libidinous, he's an unwitting acolyte for a key turning point in The Master's overarching plan. "Bolivar is a tough part, because this guy's a rock star, so you need to find someone who has enough confidence and swagger and charisma," says executive producer Carlton Cuse. "We looked at a lot of different people, then Jack Kesy came in, and he had that quality."

Dressing Bolivar, costume designer Luis Sequeira had to consider what would make him believable as a goth star. "I wanted something that

has a fantastical element to it, so we made some amazing laced leather pants," says Sequeira.

Kesy was also the only series regular to get a special kind of digital treatment for the scene in which a transforming Bolivar opens his robe to reveal that his nether regions now recall those of a doll. This was Guillermo del Toro's biological architecture of vampires made flesh, as it were. "Yeah, we had to smooth him out," says visual effects supervisor Dennis Berardi. "He wore flesh-colored underwear, but obviously his package was still in the shot, so we had to remove it."

LEFT Character concept art of Bolivar by Guy Davis.

ABOVE Gabriel Bolivar (Jack Kesy) is a rock star turned acolyte of The Master.

ABOVE Bolivar (Jack Kesy) while still under quarantine after the evacuation of Regis Air 753.

FAR LEFT Bolivar strikes a rock star pose.

LEFT and BOTTOM LEFT Posters for a Bolivar tour.

BELOW LEFT and RIGHT Jack Kesy in makeup that indicates Bolivar is succumbing to the strigoi virus.

BOTTOM RIGHT The Master prepares to transfer his consciousness to Bolivar's body.

FOLLOWING PAGES Graphic art for Gabriel Bolivar posters by Jason Graham.

BOLIVAR
2010 WORLD TOUR
JANUARY 18 · NYC

BOLIVAR

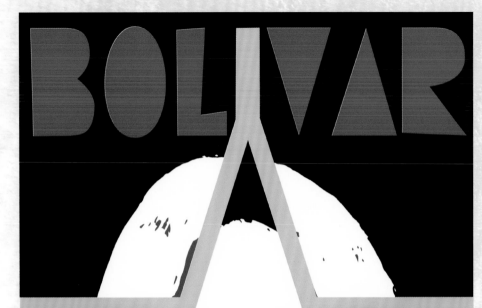

BOLIVAR

SATURDAY JANUARY 3 — ONE NIGHT NEW YORK

09 — 21

BOLIVAR
MIDNIGHT HOST

BOLIVAR'S LAIR

Fundamental to Bolivar's goth lifestyle are his gloomy quarters, situated above a concert space in an old theater called the Vestry—the idea being that Bolivar had bought a historic vaudeville space in Tribeca and turned it into his private living/performing lair. Although the stage area seen throughout the season (most notably in the finale, when the team fights a slew of vampires there) is the inside of the real Opera House rock venue in Toronto, production designer Tamara Deverell had a specific look in mind for Bolivar's bedroom. She took her cue from the legendary Gothic revival house in Toronto called Casa Loma and designed a moodily dark attic space for Bolivar's bedroom that could be built on set. Old ropes, faked theatrical tie-offs, big wood beams, and a lighting grid under the floor helped create the illusion of being above a stage, while the space's low garret windows were painted black and given an amber coating to create an eerie glow.

"Then we just went to town on the set dressing," says Deverell. "We custom-made black, shiny faux leather furniture, chandeliers, and this big round bed that we put in the middle of the room. And, because we were finally allowed to use red [since Bolivar is directly tied to The Master], we used these big red theatrical drapes and put red and black candles everywhere." A scouting mission on another project gave Deverell another idea. "I remembered that [I met a music producer who] had a bathtub just sitting in the middle of his room. It's such a rock thing to do, so I copied that in essence and put a crazy bathtub in the corner." Meanwhile, a photo shoot with Kesy provided the material to create all the posters in Bolivar's graffiti-lined bathroom, an appropriate design touch, says Deverell, "because Bolivar is in love with himself."

ABOVE Concept art for Bolivar's lair by Keith Thompson.
OPPOSITE TOP LEFT Bolivar's bathroom set featuring poster art by Jason Graham.
OPPOSITE TOP RIGHT The Bolivar boudoir set.
OPPOSITE BOTTOM Concept art for Bolivar's lair by Keith Thompson.

THE INFECTED

The normal rules of anatomy and biology simply do not apply to the vampires of Guillermo del Toro's fertile imagination: wretched creatures who completely transform their conquered human hosts inside and out. From the nasty stream of bloodworms, which starts the process inside a victim, to the gruesome terror of a full-on strigoi in assault mode, it's a vicious circle of unnatural corruption. Realizing this army of evil required an army of artists—painters, sculptors, makeup crews, actors, and dancers—who, working together, gave this decimating scourge its dark visual richness.

VAMPIRE BIOLOGY 101

GUILLERMO DEL TORO'S VAMPIRES aren't avatars for the ache of romantic love or societally minded citizens with a well-honed taste for seduction. They're literally monsters, hungry for blood, animalistic in their need, and with a method of reproduction that's viral. They're genuinely diseased, and they look it. Because of that, what makes them fascinating creatures is as much what happens on the inside as how they appear on the outside.

For *The Strain* to properly reintroduce the world to genuinely scary vampires, del Toro sought to create a violently convulsive biological process to match the chaotic change they wreak in the world. From that first explicitly violent attack in the pilot episode when a hideous proboscis emerges from the darkness of The Master's cloaked hood and leeches the blood from Bishop, it was clear that this was going to be a forensic vampire show, unafraid to go gorily anatomical.

Guillermo del Toro had each of the stages of vampirism mapped out from the start and was able to provide the crew with an astonishing amount

of detail on the entire process. What happens, for example, when you get bitten by a strigoi and the parasitic bloodworms they release go to town on your physiology?

"Your metabolism accelerates rapidly, as the new organs efficiently take over the old organs," says del Toro. "You get a huge fever, because your basal temperature rises and rises. Your hair falls out all at once or little by little. You get an incredibly sore throat as the stinger starts to fuse the parasitic organs into one single unit. You get chest cramps as bone spurs form to propel the stinger. Your digestive system starts to simplify. You basically evacuate your system. You stop eating, and you start disposing of the food really rapidly. Then all your soft tissue 'down there' falls off: testicles, penis, anything that is not useful, because none of the strigoi reproduce genetically."

PREVIOUS PAGES Marketing artwork for season two of *The Strain*.

THIS PAGE Concept art of the stinger and a strigoi transformation by Guy Davis.

RIGHT Photoshopped stages of strigoi transformation by Chris Devitt.

STAGE 0

STAGE 1

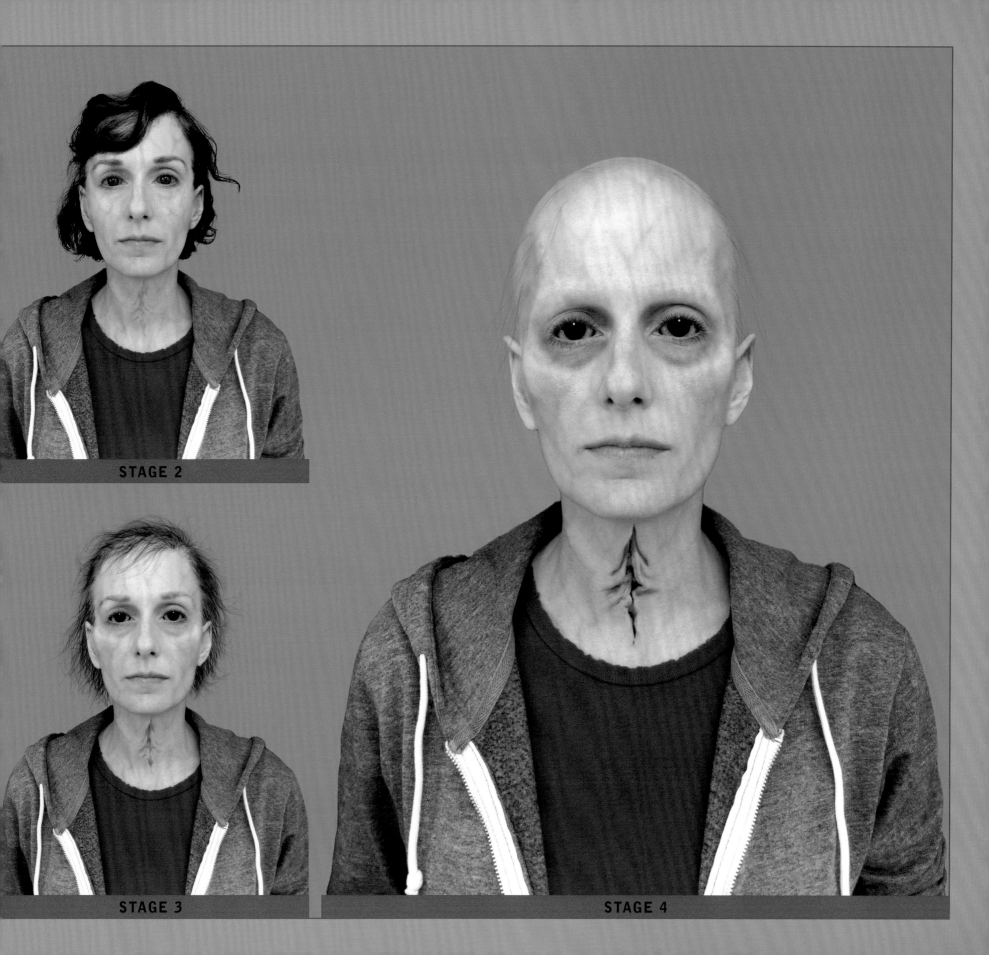

STAGE 2

STAGE 3

STAGE 4

On that last, particularly graphic stage, del Toro elaborates, drawing from his longstanding study of entomology: "Basically, there are certain types of insects that become so specialized that some of them are born without sexual organs or without a mouth. They're meant to be laborers that last a certain amount of time. They do their job and die. The idea with these creatures is that none of them are going to screw. None will reproduce that way. So it all goes away."

Unfortunately for the infected, the indignities do not end there, as del Toro explains further: "Then, your anus and genitals fuse into one opening, and you just basically get a very ugly looking orifice down there. Because your lungs die and you cease breathing, what happens with your internal organs is they all feed the growth that becomes the stinger, and your digestive system becomes highly simplified. You become like a tick. You are shitting as you eat, because you don't retain any food. That's why the 777 was full of stains. The Master was disposing of ammonia and plasma while he was drinking the passengers' blood. And, if you notice, The Master actually has huge shit stains on his robes."

This meticulously designed interior makeover isn't explicitly documented in the show, but nevertheless, the transformation needed to be physically represented via the outward appearance of the infected to suggest that this was a gradual process. The Master and Eichhorst are, of course, two of the most fully developed vampires featured prominently in the first season, which covers a period of just over a week, from the initial outbreak to the vampire hunters' showdown with The Master. As a result, most of the vampires in season one, from the Regis Air passengers onward, are freshly "turned" and only in the first stages of metamorphosis. Between prosthetics, makeup, and movement, a clear gradation of the transformation process needed to be put into effect for the entire series.

The production came up with four stages, initially as a hair-and-makeup/prosthetics guide. The infection begins with a discoloration of the skin, some veining, and the reddening of the eyes,

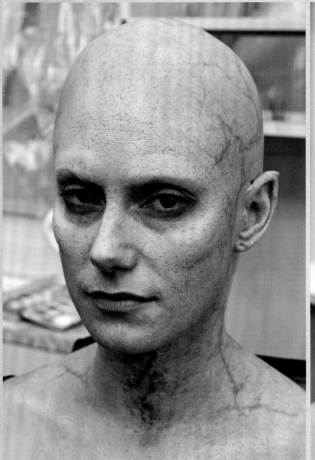

OPPOSITE Actress Natalie Brown as Kelly Goodweather in an early stage of strigoi transformation.

FAR LEFT AND LEFT Brown undergoes an extensive makeup process to play Kelly.

ABOVE Brown as Kelly Goodweather on set.

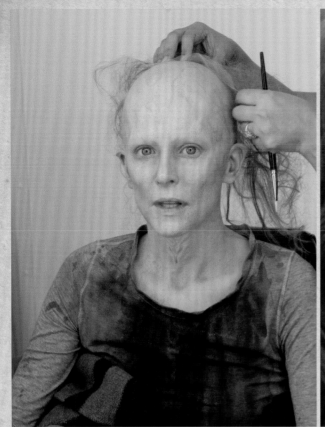

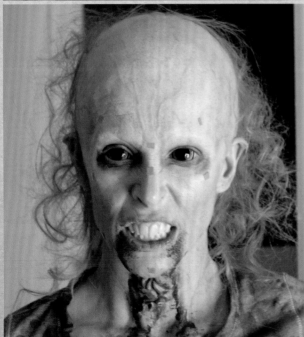

TOP LEFT Applying makeup to actress Leslie Hope so she can play Joan Luss in the late stages of her infection.

TOP RIGHT Makeup artists had their work cut out for them on the set of *The Strain*.

ABOVE Joan (Leslie Hope) in full strigoi glory with orange markers for VFX reference

OPPOSITE PAGE Production photos of made-up strigoi background players in various stages of transformation.

characteristics that the makeup department can create easily. "People who are first infected, they just look pale and balmy," says Steve Newburn, whose creature shop department helped with stage two and beyond, when fleshy prosthetic applications that required prep work were needed. "Second stage, the eyes are bloodshot, and you see ruptured blood vessels, and very subtle veins are starting to appear through the skin. The skin becomes more translucent, and a tiny little hint of a wattle appears on the neck."

There's also a slight bit of hair loss and brown stains down the fronts of shirts because, as producer J. Miles Dale puts it, "they're in the process of biomorphing, so they puke on themselves." Costume designer Luis Sequeira and his crew are responsible for aging the clothes of the strigoi. (After being infected, victims no longer feel the need to change their outfits or bathe, of course.) For that process, chemicals applied by Sequeira's team broke down the fibers of the clothes. They also applied solutions meant to represent bodily fluids. "We have bottles of liquid that say 'Vomit' or 'Blood,'" says Sequeira. "We just start laying that in, and at one point near the end of the first season, when there are oodles of vampires, we had an assembly line going."

It's at stage three that the hair of the infected actually begins falling out in patches. Newburn says the look is reminiscent of the hair loss suffered by chemotherapy patients: "Also, the wattle starts to really appear, the veins are more pronounced, and the skin's gotten really pale."

Stage four sees the most advanced version of the season one strigoi emerge: a hairless look in which the wattle is now distinct. Newburn says that wattles are different depending on one's time as a vampire—basically, the longer the victim has been infected, the bigger the wattle gets. When they began creating wattles in the shop for newly turned vamps, the color resembled the paleness of the skin. "But over time, Guillermo asked that they take on an irritated tone, like a bad rash," says Newburn. "That lasts for some time—decades. Once you get into The Master and the various strigoi that are centuries old, the wattles start to become almost like blood sacs, with blood pooling into the lowest points."

Newburn notes that as fearsome as the stage four strigoi is, it's only the beginning of the transformation. "It's going to go a lot further, ultimately," he says. "It's just going to take a while to get there, because you can't spill all the beans in the first season and have nowhere to go."

VAMP CAMP

WHILE MANY DIFFERENT DEPARTMENTS worked at perfecting the surface appearance of the strigoi, attention also turned to addressing their monstrous movements. Striving to avoid comparisons to zombie-like lurching, accomplished choreographer Roberto Campanella was hired to initiate a master class in strigoi movement, which the crew affectionately tagged "vamp camp." Using this method, each performer set to appear as a strigoi would undergo rigorous and regimented training that would leave them with a unified approach to the movement of the infected characters.

For stages one and two, when the infection is just making itself felt, the ambulatory change isn't as apparent. "You're just shuffling along and not really in control," says producer J. Miles Dale. "You're basically kind of confused. It's transitional." Movement in stages three and four, on the other hand, needed to vividly communicate that the strigoi are hunters with a threatening animalistic intelligence, connected to each other telepathically, as if working in a pack. Some might crawl, others might scamper; head turns carry a hyperawareness, while torsos become more arched and fingers continuously move to suggest coursing bloodworms. Also impacting movement is the six-foot stinger concealed within the body of the strigoi. This grim organ triggers a different kind of posture when a vampire begins to attack.

"Counterweighting the stinger is important," says Dale. "You've got to get some stability, because that stinger is not light, and there's a leveraging

effect. One foot's in front, and one's in back, and the hands go back. It's understanding the physics of it."

It's probably not surprising to learn that along with stunt people and lead actors, professional dancers, trained in movement, comprise a large section of the strigoi hoard. "Anyone who's just moving and snarling, they're dancers," says Dale. "We wanted to codify these movements, and dancers were the best way to do that, so we have a pretty good repertory company." Changing each dancer's makeup, hair, and wardrobe from episode to episode allows the production to reuse the dancers without drawing viewers' attention to the duplication. Some of the male dancers were even willing to shave their heads to help facilitate different looks over the season.

Ruta Gedmintas, who plays Dutch Velders, marvels at the work of the vampire performers. "It's really creepy to watch what looks like a human descend into this pure animal instinct of just hunger," says Gedmintas. "They really capture

that in the movement. These huge [groups] of vampires would come running at you, and they're so good with their movements, I didn't have to do any acting because I was terrified!"

Miguel Gomez, who plays Gus, says the overall look of the vampires is so effective he makes a point of staying away from the vamp actors before shooting so he can react more authentically when the cameras roll. "Then I can look at them as if this was really happening, and it's sort of scary," he says. "You look in their eyes that have been blacked out and made extremely red, and that loss of consciousness is a scary thing. They just want to eat. They look soulless."

OPPOSITE Strigoi emerge from a shipping container in season one.

ABOVE An infected Dr. Bennett (Jeffrey R. Smith) runs amok on the streets of New York.

ABOVE RIGHT A background player crouches in a typical strigoi pose.

99

STRENGTH IN NUMBERS

WITH THE SHEER NUMBER of vampires set to rise in future seasons of *The Strain*, producer J. Miles Dale knew it would be tough for the vampire-creating crew to support that kind of volume, so some advance work served to lighten the load: "[For season two we] made at least fifty high-quality masks for background vampires, the ones who aren't in the front row. You pull on the mask, tuck it into the wardrobe, do some touch-ups and clean the hair, and you can get away with that. You just can't afford to spend four hours on every one of them when there might be twenty-five extras. There were days on the first season when I had eight makeup and five hair artists for the extras. You just can't survive that."

In one key instance during season one, the digital effects team provided the added vampires needed, a number that Vasiliy Fet roughly describes during the scene as "a *lot* of munchers." This was the striking moment at the end of episode

eleven, "The Third Rail," when the hunting team of Fet, Setrakian, Eph, and Nora hit upon a narrow passageway in the tunnels leading to a space that, upon illumination by a flare, reveals a jaw-dropping horde of nesting strigoi.

Visual effects supervisor Dennis Berardi of Mr. X Inc. says that of the one-thousand-plus shots his team worked on during the first season of

The Strain, this was one of the most complex, because it involved layered photography in which separate shots are arranged over each other to create one image. "Guillermo wanted to treat the moment like a reveal," says Berardi. "There's a close-up on the reaction, and we see what they see, their point of view. He wanted vamps right in the immediate foreground and sprawling throughout the tunnel—two, three, four thousand—as many as we could fit in there."

The creation of the shot began with a digital pre-visualization animation incorporating a virtual version of the lens that would be utilized during filming. "We modeled every lens being used on the production," says Berardi. "So, for example, my computer's 25-mm lens shows exactly what their 25-mm lens will do on a set." After discussing the framing of the image, Berardi knew how many foreground strigoi would have to be filmed. The master shot was then physically captured on a

set with twenty actors in strigoi makeup against a green screen. "On a separate day," continues Berardi, "we shot elements of strigoi in various positions in a matched camera angle against a green screen, so they could be composited and we could tile them." He also filmed texture references of the underground subway where the scene is set. Lastly, the teeming, distant background vampires were created digitally. "There were probably about ten layered elements, and I think it came together quite well," he says.

When dealing with a pressurized television schedule, being well prepared is essential. Berardi scours each script in advance—he typically receives it one month before the episode shoots—spots the potentially complicated moments and begins working on them as soon as he can. "Although there are different directors on different episodes, Guillermo's the ultimate authority," says Berardi. "I work things out first and then show him, and if he agrees, I start making a shooting plan. When we show up on the set for a complicated shot, it's just about execution. I've got my pre-viz, I've told all the department heads how I want to shoot it, so we're not inventing on the day. It's a very tight shooting schedule as well. We can't be messing around."

OPPOSITE TOP LEFT AND OPPOSITE MIDDLE A final shot of thousands of strigoi underground and the original shot featuring live-action performers against a green screen, which was digitally augmented to add background and hundreds of digital vamps.

OPPOSITE TOP RIGHT Another digitally augmented strigoi attack.

THIS PAGE Before and after comparison images show how Mr. X subtly added digital strigoi to two major scenes.

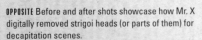

BEHEADINGS

THE SUREST WAY TO KILL A VAMPIRE, as frequently demonstrated by Abraham Setrakian, is to behead it. It's not as easy as it looks, though—at least for those who have to create these bloodily brutal moments. For one thing, every beheading is done with a digital blade. The first step requires play-acting with a non-existent sword. Setrakian actor David Bradley uses a stunt prop that consists of just a hilt with a four-inch blade featuring a marked tip to indicate where the rest of the sword will be added digitally. He then swings at his intended victim, judging where his foe's neck will meet the blade, and the receiving actor drops to the ground.

"Everything is prepared, everyone rehearsed properly, so you don't find yourself improvising on screen in a take," says Bradley. "You know the distances."

"We recheck the take in playback to make sure that the swing and the actor's reaction on the receiving end are roughly in synch," says visual effects supervisor Dennis Berardi. "Then we shoot a clean plate [a shot with no strigoi actor, just background] because I have to digitally sever the head, and animate it off, and reveal the background. It's actually quite a process, because if the reaction on the receiving end is a second too soon or too late, it just doesn't work. We're pretty good about identifying any problems with timing on set, though, so if it happens, you go again with another take." After that, if a prosthetic head is needed to complete the sequence—for example, the one that comes flying down the stairs of Gus's family's apartment building in season one, episode eleven, "The Third Rail," the creature shop artists provide a dummy head, filled with white goo.

Though the beheadings are often exciting bits of action in the series, they've also reflected the story's more affecting elements, too, as when Mia Maestro's character Nora Martinez had to decapitate her own mother, who had been tragically turned by a strigoi. "It was quite emotional," says Maestro, "and one of the hardest things I had to do in terms of preparation, because it was emotional *and* technical."

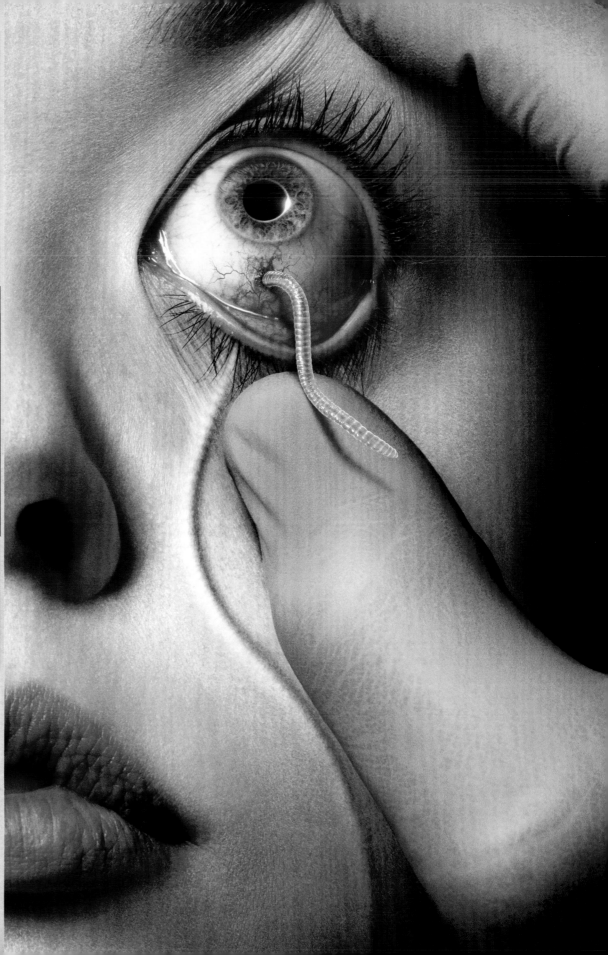

ABOVE, TOP TO BOTTOM Digitally created bloodworms as seen in final frames from *The Strain*.

RIGHT Provocative poster art for season one of *The Strain*.

OPPOSITE LEFT Before and after shots of tweezers removing a bloodworm, with the creature digitally added to complete the shot.

OPPOSITE RIGHT A green synthetic prop heart is digitally enhanced to include ravaging bloodworms.

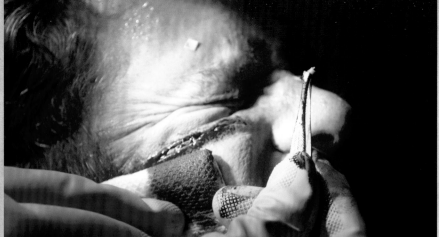

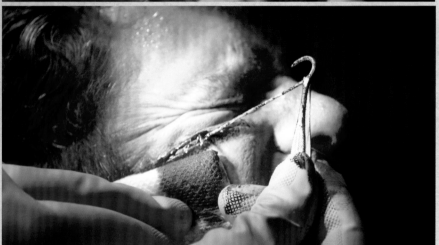

BLOODWORMS

Guillermo del Toro created bloodworms that invade the body and spread the vampiric sickness as a way to scientifically manifest the idea that strigoi are truly an epidemic, a corrupting evil that literally gets under the skin. (Squirmy, parasitic horsehair worms were an inspiration for del Toro.) Guy Davis worked on the pilot episode storyboards that depicted the medical examiner Bennett getting attacked. Despite the scene being full of shocks, not least of all the sight of an undead character in mid-autopsy with her internal organs in full view, it was the bloodworms that really sent shivers up the spine. "That to me was creepier than anything else," he says.

In order for Dennis Berardi to successfully create the digital bloodworms that Bennett frantically tries to pull from beneath the skin of his hand, a sophisticated lighting and rendering technique was employed called subsurface scattering. "If you hold your hand to a light, some of the light is reflected, but some of it is absorbed and scatters underneath the surface of the skin, because your skin can be translucent," says Berardi. "So our challenge was to make that look photo-real and put the worm into that environment. We had all these versions where the hand was too opaque, it was too reflective, too shiny, and then all these takes where we were too absorptive with the light, and it was starting to look too translucent."

Through the iterative process that Berardi subscribes to, in which take after take is shown to del Toro and adjustments are made, a partly digital hand was eventually created that matched the feeling of the photographed, live-action hand. "In the end, it made for an effective, fun scene," says Berardi.

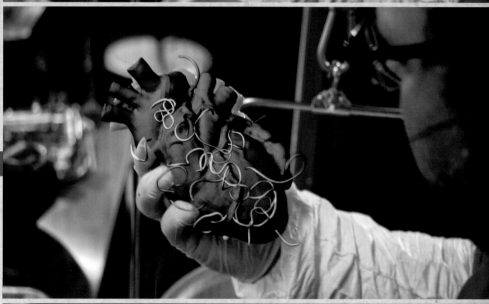

THESE PAGES Bloodworm concept art by Keith Thompson.

THE STINGER

IN ATTACK MODE, the vampires of *The Strain* have a ferocious weapon at their disposal: the tool del Toro calls "the stinger" that ejects from the strigoi's mouth, latching onto their prey and sucking out the blood. It's an appendage that Guillermo del Toro has been adapting and refining on what he calls a "trial and error" basis for years. "Originally it was going to be in *Cronos*, but I didn't have the budget," says del Toro. "Then I tried it on *Blade II*, but it felt small and didn't do what I wanted. Then I tried it on *Hellboy* with Sammael, and I learned a lot on what to do and what not to do, and all that came to play on *The Strain*. It's the best stinger I've ever done."

The development of the stinger began in the concept art stage with Simon Lee working on sculpts of The Master in which the deadly appendage resembled a tail coming from the mouth. Something seemed lacking, though. Guy Davis suggested the stinger be forked, with a part that can wrap around the neck so that the stinger can act like a needle. "It's the tooth that would stab into the neck," says Davis. "It looked obscene, too, which I always think is good for making something even creepier." With del Toro frequently giving his input throughout the process, the final stinger for the show was approved, the central defining feature being its spider-like pincer that comes out of the mouth and then splits to reveal even more disturbing details.

The next question to address was whether the complex design of the stinger could be implemented as a physical special effect. Typically, del Toro's mantra is that you should do what you can in-camera until you can't progress further, at which point you turn to digital effects. Although the team made every effort to find physical solutions to each problem, at times—as in the case of the animatronic Master torso created by Steve Newburn and Sean Sansom—the digital option was best. Says Newburn, "Trying to do that from a puppetry standpoint, it's time-consuming, and

when you're on a show as ambitious as this is, where you're on an eight-day schedule for an episode, it's not sensible to spend several hours trying to catch a stinger shooting out at somebody when you can deal with it later through CG."

Dennis Berardi of visual effects company Mr. X Inc. recalls the early discussions he had with del Toro about how the stinger would be depicted as a dimensional object. Berardi suggested creating a screen test to provide proof of concept for the effect. In the lobby of the Mr. X headquarters, a makeshift post-apocalyptic set was created, and an animator

ABOVE Concept art of a stinger projecting by Guy Davis.

RIGHT Concept art of a stinger organ autopsy by Guy Davis and Simon Webber.

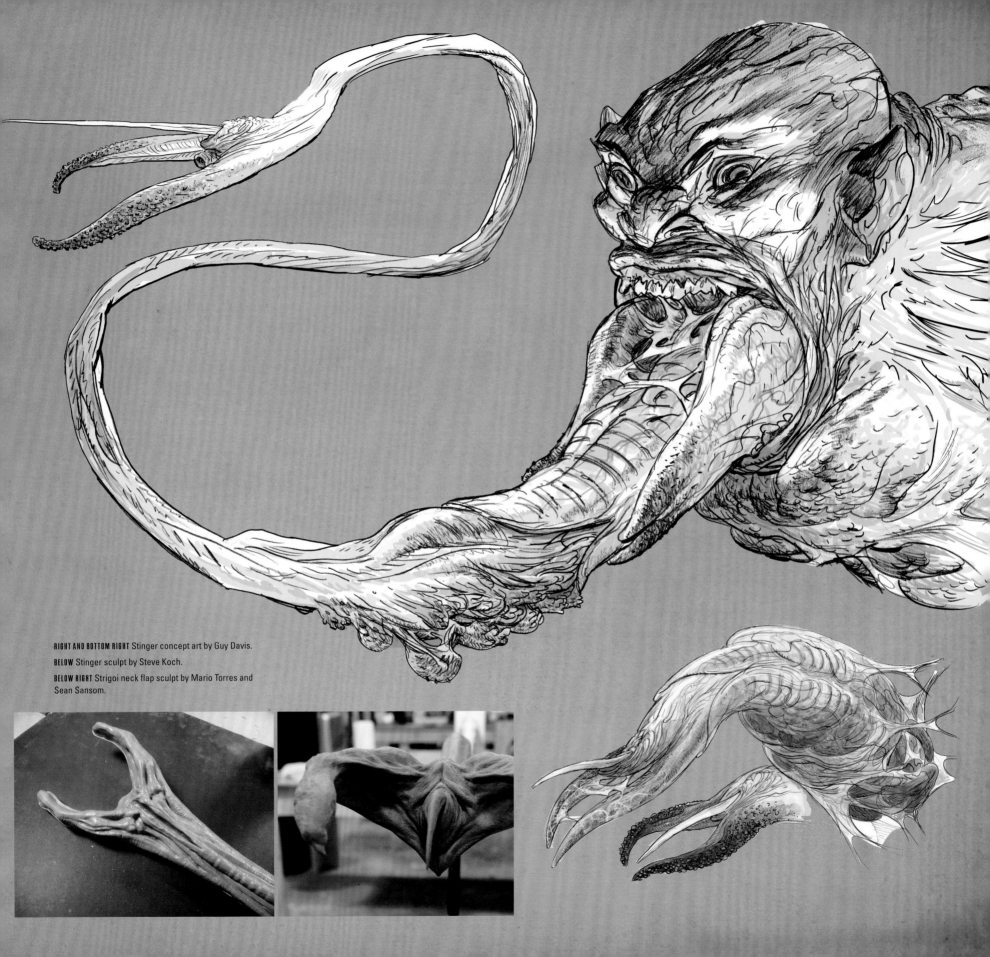

RIGHT AND BOTTOM RIGHT Stinger concept art by Guy Davis.

BELOW Stinger sculpt by Steve Koch.

BELOW RIGHT Strigoi neck flap sculpt by Mario Torres and Sean Sansom.

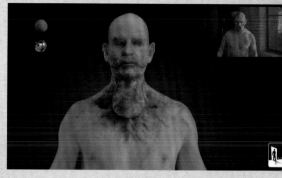

was tapped to don strigoi makeup and act out the part, his body dotted with tracking markers. The finished shot was then imported into the company's 3-D software, and the actor was given a drastic digital makeover. Most of the performer's face and jaw were replaced, a stinger was added, and del Toro quickly signed off on the effect. "He loved it," says Berardi. "He could see that it worked visually."

When it came time to film scenes that would need to be augmented with a digital stinger, Berardi's little research-and-development project had shown him that the best way to showcase the stingers was to get the physical shoot right in the first place—in particular, to keep the shots with the actors from looking too staged or too flatly lit: "It's a bit of a paradigm shift in recent years in visual effects, where we used to require that cameras not move so much and lighting be flat and that it be lensed a certain way, so the CG could be put into it. We've really moved away from that process."

BELOW AND RIGHT Before and after shots of Nora getting attacked by a strigoi, with the stinger digitally added.

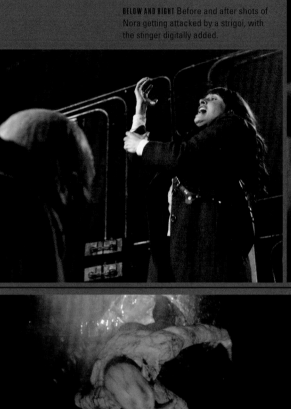

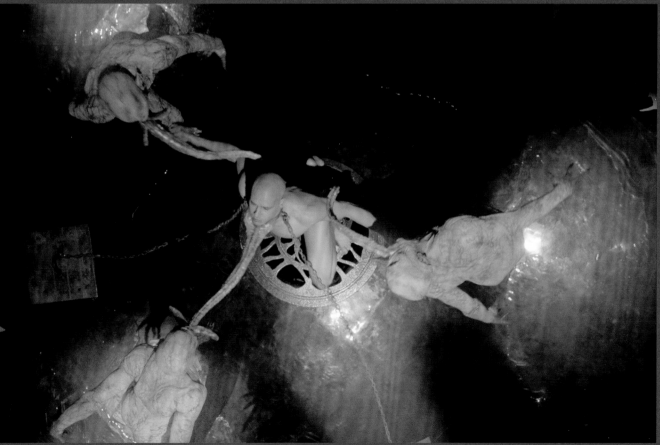

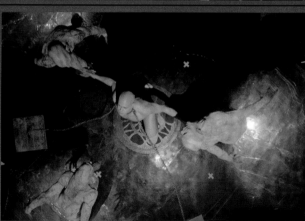

ABOVE AND LEFT The Ancients assault their prey, with their stingers added digitally.

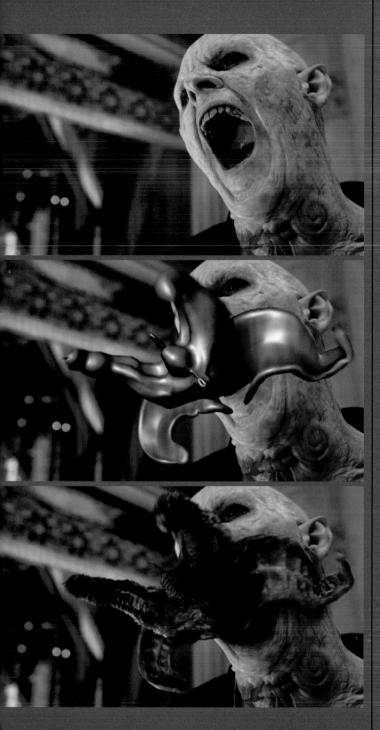

THIS PAGE Further examples illustrate the process of adding computer-enhanced strigoi effects to live-action shots of strigoi performers.

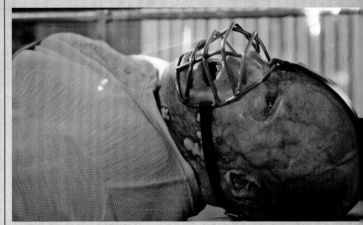

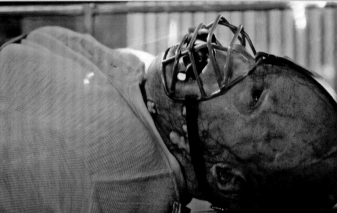

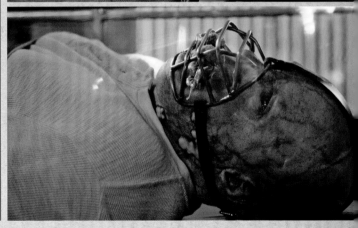

On set, Berardi's direction to crew and actors is to keep in mind that the stinger can extend six feet, as there needs to be enough space between vampire and intended victim for the effect to be added in. Also important is giving the actor or actors an eyeline for the stinger. "I usually stage the action as if it was really happening," he says. "I always encourage them to be aggressive with the camera, light the scene moodily, and really get a performance, as if this fleshy stinger was coming out of the actors' mouths. The most successful stinger shots are where the actor really sells it, the camera's moving, and it's lit real moody. Then the CG animation integrates right in."

The effects artists at Mr. X Inc. also had to keep in mind that stingers differ from vamp to vamp, depending on what stage the person is at in the transformation process. Says Berardi, "The Master's stinger has these nodules on it, developed over a thousand years, and his stinger is more leathery and detailed, more muscular. If it's a young strigoi, like you see with the little girl, Emma, when she's in the bathtub, it's really pink and not developed. It doesn't have the nodules or the gnarled, textured surface. The barbs aren't as developed. Those are the two extremes. We also scale the stingers appropriately to the size of the actors. You have to believe it came out of that throat."

TOP AND ABOVE Stingers added to a strigoi attack scene from the season two episode "The Assassin."

RIGHT One of Eph's infected test subjects before and after the digital stinger is added.

THE AUTOPSY

ALTHOUGH THE MAJORITY of the stingers were created digitally, there were a few instances when actors got to see an art department–created stinger on set, one that thankfully wasn't flying through the air at them. These non-articulated pieces were created for scenes where the appendage could appear limp, such as moments involving dead strigoi. For example, when Gus, his buddy Felix, and Jim Kent are dealing with the disposal of infected Captain Redfern's body, there's a moment when Felix opens up the bag, and a slimy-looking stinger, a silicone creation courtesy of the creature shop, falls out. "That thing looked like an octopus tentacle," says actor Miguel Gomez. "I mean, it was disgusting!"

Redfern's disposal comes after his death by fire extinguisher and subsequent autopsy conducted by Eph and Nora, who come face to face—or rather face to innards—with the reality of the threat they're up against. Featured in season one, episode four, aptly titled "It's Not For Everyone," the show-stopping scene brings home the stomach-turning intricacy of the strigoi anatomy developed by del Toro.

For his part, del Toro knows that he has a reputation for biological thoroughness when it comes

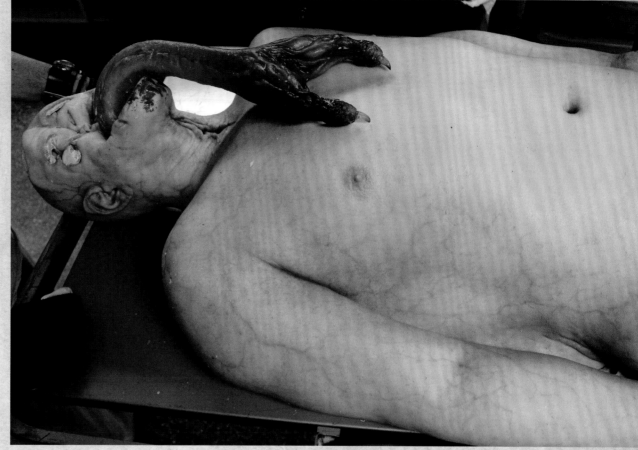

to his monsters. "Jim Cameron makes fun of me, saying I'm unable to resist having an autopsy in every one of my movies, and to a point he's right," says del Toro. "Out of nine features I've done, at least six contain an autopsy of some form. But the way I feel is, there's a tacit agreement with the audience that if you can produce a corpse, you've made them believe a creature was alive."

Del Toro likens the impact of an autopsy scene to the debates that surround cryptozoology: "Everybody is waiting for someone to analyze the body of a Sasquatch or a chupacabra, you know? The moment you produce the creature, there's a belief that it's real. So I think autopsies are very useful in that you open the clockwork and see the gears inside the clock. It's biologically fascinating."

The actor portraying Eph, Corey Stoll, agrees with del Toro, calling the autopsy scene "brilliant." He adds, "In history, the power for vampires has always been in their mystery. Here was a vampire

laid naked as possible, and it was a great way to turn the whole myth on its head."

Prepping the autopsy scene began in the concept art stage. Guy Davis worked on drawings that would show how a six-foot stinger fit inside a cadaver after the body's various internal mutations. He then passed on those renderings to 3D modeler Simon Webber. "Simon does amazing ZBrush work," says Davis, referring to the digital sculpting tool that in this case was used to give contour and shape to the dead vampire's insides. "Fully rendered, it looked realistic and disgusting, and that's when we knew we did it right."

Following that stage, creature shop artists Sean Sansom and Steve Newburn made a lifecast of actor Jonathan Potts, who plays Redfern, and

OPPOSITE Strigoi autopsy concept art by Guy Davis.

LEFT Concept art of a blacklight strigoi autopsy by Simon Webber.

ABOVE Body mould of actor Jonathan Potts as the autopsied Redfern, with prosthetic stinger protruding.

then created body molds from the cast. Next, an outer skin and muscle layer was fashioned, as well as an inner cavity for the internal organs, which were built out of extremely soft, heavily plasticized silicone with vinyl and latex layers. The rib cage was constructed out of fiberglass and dressed with silicone to look authentically visceral. Body fluids were then added by using many layers of a tinted gel called Ultra Ice. Since the scene required the stinger to be pulled out through the esophagus, the fake throat piece had to be made of softer silicone so it could stretch to three or four times its size. The stinger itself—a smaller version of the one seen coming out of The Master in the pilot—had to be hidden inside the intestinal area, so it wouldn't be readily visible upon opening the body.

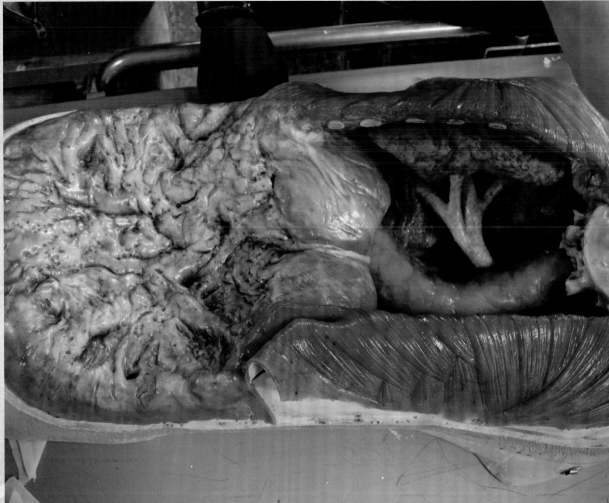

ABOVE Actor Jonathan Potts in the process of getting a lifecast.

Knowing the stinger would be pulled out and dissected onscreen, Sansom and Newburn sculpted an inner skeleton layered in silicone tendons and muscles and created a two-and-a-half-inch-long stinger barb. The entire assembly was then loaded into a thin stinger skin that could then be cut open during filming and peeled open to reveal the innards. "It all had the same feel as pulling the meat out of crab legs," says Newburn.

For the purposes of reducing the amount of prep time, only one fully functional Redfern corpse was created. To further expedite the process, Sansom and Newburn built a hatch in the back of the corpse that would allow crew to access the body and reset the insides if a second take was needed. With this mechanism in place, the only concern from a resetting standpoint was the shot of the scalpel cutting the skin for the first time. If it needed to be redone, the incision would have to be digitally erased. (Fortunately, they got it right the first time.)

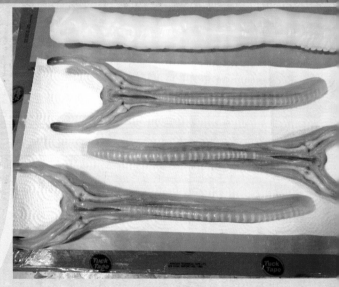

TOP Strigoi autopsy organs created by the creature effects team.

ABOVE Disembodied stingers for the autopsy scene.

OPPOSITE TOP The Redfern lifecast splayed open with prosthetic organs visible.

OPPOSITE INSET From the autopsy scene, an infected heart with parasitic tumors.

Meanwhile, tubes inside the body were also inserted to pump in the white goo-blood prevalent in all of del Toro's vampires. The goo is made from a food thickener that starts as powder until water is added. "Depending on how much water or powder you use, you can have everything from water consistency to full blown sludge," says Newburn. "A lot of the goo in other scenes is CG. It's pretty rare to do on-set gunshots with [practical] blood effects anymore. But with a body like this, it makes sense to do it, because we can just have it oozing in there, then mop it out and do it again. It's pretty quick and easy."

Stoll says filming the autopsy was one of those instances when very little imagination had to be used on his part. "It was our first real encounter with the incredible work being done by the creature shop," he says. "Everything was workable. That tongue really was curled up inside that cavity. We cut through a first layer of skin, and there was this fat and muscle layer, and then we had to cut through that with these shears, and then there were these organs that were incredibly detailed and layered. I've never encountered anything like that before."

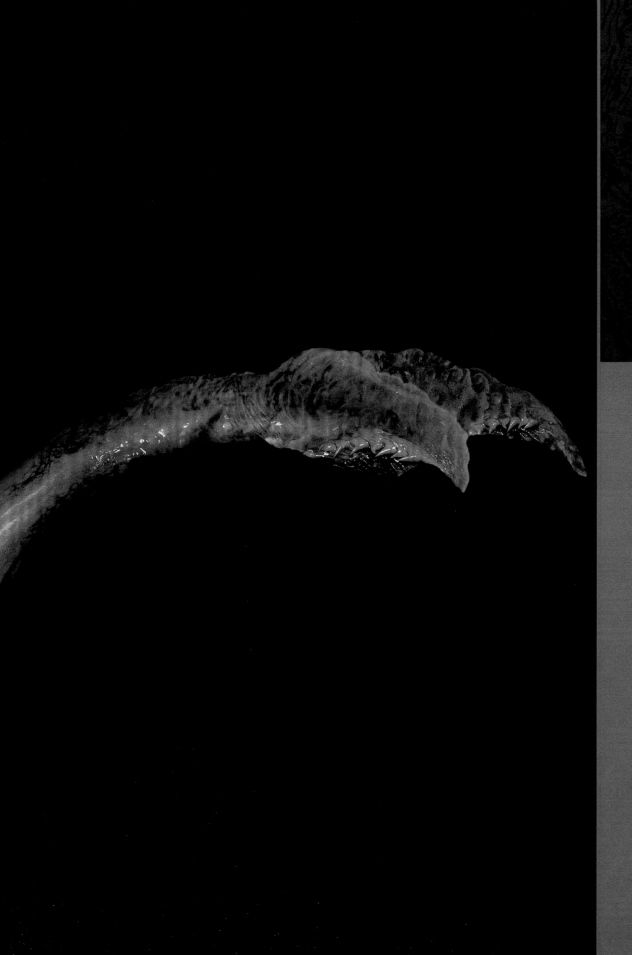

IT SPREADS

SEASON ONE OF *The Strain* ended with its intrepid band of vampire hunters in a state of edgy limbo. The Master was cornered at Bolivar's theater but managed to escape in broad daylight. Young Zack Goodweather was traumatized by encountering his infected mother and then seeing his dad try to kill her. The last shot saw the team making its way across the Brooklyn Bridge, pockets of fires ravaging a transforming Manhattan in the background.

When planning season two, the producers and writers saw an opportunity to expand the scope of the show beyond what happens in the novels and turn it into what Chuck Hogan calls "season 2.0."

SEASON TWO

"WE STEPPED IT UP," says Hogan. "It's almost as if with season one, we got this present, we unwrapped it, we looked at it and said, 'Wow.' With season two, it was: 'Let's play with this thing.'"

Season two of *The Strain* saw the show's creators expanding the narrative. Carlton Cuse, Chuck Hogan, and the writers worked to add new characters and storylines that would show the fall of our society. Most post-apocalyptic shows begin after the end of the world, but The Strain is unique in illustrating how that decline of civilization happens. "We planned it like that," says del Toro. "[There are] bigger, more brutal, more massive attacks in the second season."

"The world has changed," says producer J. Miles Dale. "Whereas it was isolated incidents in season one, [in season two] the stakes are bigger. There's the National Guard, Hummers, soldiers, helicopters, and lots and lots of vampires."

New York's implosion, and the widespread realization that a plague is in full swing, became the churning backdrop for season two, and it necessitated dramatic storylines that explored characters in action, instead of reaction. Setrakian, emboldened by his attack on The Master, takes up the search for the *Occido Lumen*, a book of ancient lore that could hold the key to stopping his nemesis. Eph, Nora, and Fet—using Fet's warehouse digs as a new base of operations—work at coming up with a bioweapon to infect the infected. With the help of a strong-willed Staten Island politician, they all fight to make the Brooklyn neighborhood of Red Hook a vampire-free zone, leading to an all-out confrontation between strigoi and humans.

Meanwhile, the forces of evil are not resting easy either. Eph's ex-wife Kelly Goodweather, a freshly turned vampire, has picked up her own creepy acolytes; Thomas Eichhorst continues to scheme to secure his standing with The Master; no longer a terminally ill recluse, Eldritch Palmer has started buying factories as part of The Master's grim next step toward domination; and The Master himself—wounded after his showdown with Setrakian—has put in motion the next phase of his ongoing survival.

"There's a high degree of invention in season two," says Dale. "It just got bigger."

PREVIOUS PAGES Marketing art created for season two of *The Strain*.

LEFT Dutch (Ruta Gedmintas) in the gym strigoi attack from the season two episode "By Any Means."

ABOVE New York City is in lockdown in the wake of the strigoi invasion.

OPPOSITE Marketing art created for season two of *The Strain*. Note that the strigoi teeth form the Manhattan skyline.

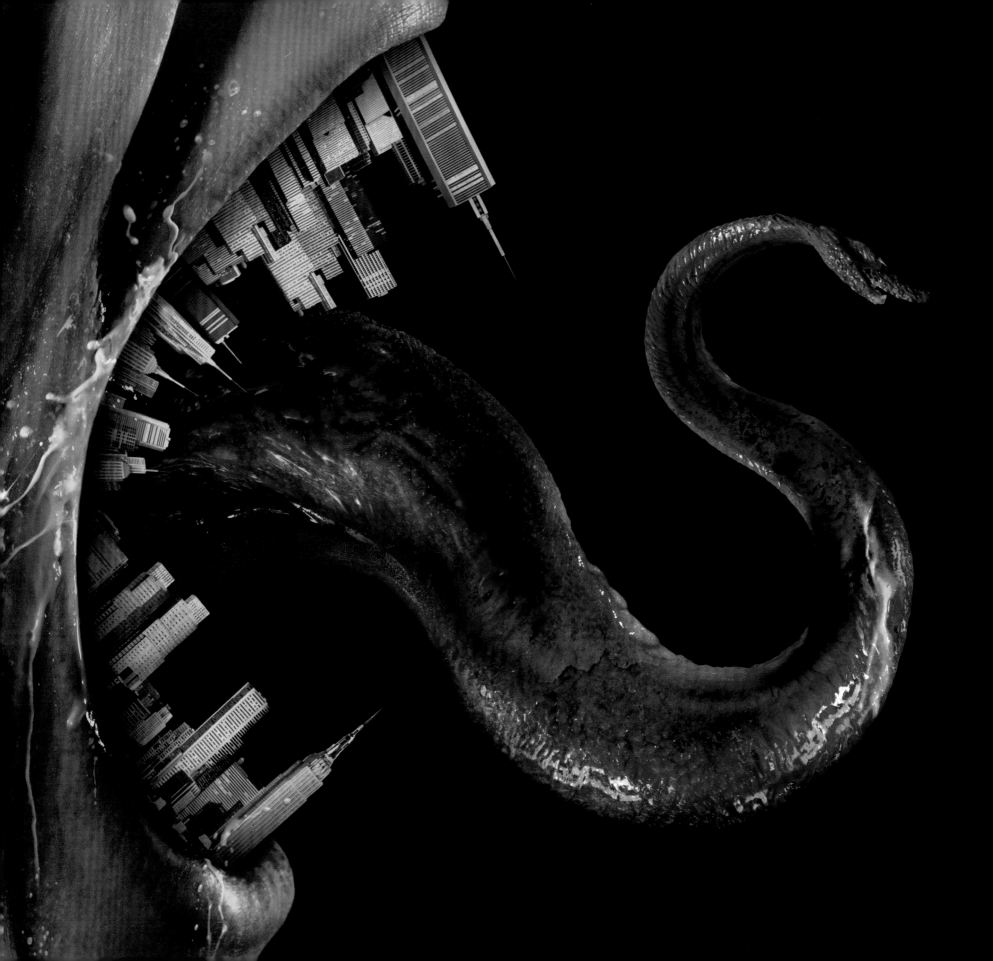

CASTING FORWARD

SEASON TWO INTRODUCED major new characters, some pulled directly from del Toro's and Hogan's books, others created in the writers' room, but all of them adding rich new dimensions to the war between humans and strigoi.

At the end of season one, viewers were led into a cavernous subterranean chamber that held a regal set of decrepit strigoi elders known as The Ancients, each perched on standing thrones with ominous puddles of blood on the floor beneath them. In their struggle against The Master—essentially a fellow Ancient whose self-serving, megalomaniacal actions run contrary to their desire to remain a hidden vampire community—this sinister-looking trio recruited Gus to become their champion warrior or Sun Hunter. "The Ancients don't propagate their own species," says Chuck Hogan. "They'll feed and kill so it doesn't spread, so they aren't discovered. But they've created these hunters—you can think of them as palace guards—to protect their living space."

In conceiving The Ancients' look, del Toro had mummies in mind, shriveled beings whose skins resemble dried fruit. "I wanted them very compressed, their hands across their chest, their legs bound together, the texture of their skin like wrinkle upon wrinkle upon wrinkle," says del Toro. "I wanted it to be impossible to imagine them living but then a shock when they finally moved. They also needed to be theatrically displayed in an operatic layout, a semicircle." The creature shop added a touch of directional marbling to The Ancients' body suits as well, with the two figures on the sides featuring skin marbling that points toward the center Ancient. "It's a very artistic little dynamic," says creature shop supervisor Steve Newburn. "You wouldn't necessarily notice it, but it's there."

OPPOSITE Keyframe art of The Ancients by Keith Thompson with Guy Davis.
ABOVE Gus (Miguel Gomez) in The Ancients' lair.
INSET Drain design for The Ancients' chamber by Matt Morgan.

LEFT Computer rendering of The Ancients' thrones by Matthew Morgan.

BOTTOM LEFT The Ancients with Gus (Miguel Gomez) and two Sun Hunters.

ABOVE Full-size concept sculpts of The Ancients, made by Carol Koch.

OPPOSITE Actors Doug Jones, Clayton Scott, and Tyler Webb play The Ancients.

OPPOSITE Concept art of the Sun Hunters by Keith Thompson.

TOP LEFT Vaun (Stephen McHattie) surrounded by slain strigoi.

TOP RIGHT AND ABOVE The Sun Hunters invade Palmer's apartment with dire consequences in the episode "Fort Defiance."

FAR LEFT Sun Hunter emblem concepts by Guy Davis.

CENTER Head cast of Stephen McHattie, who plays Vaun.

LEFT McHattie in the process of being made up to play Vaun.

The first Sun Hunter viewers met was the crossbow-wielding vampire who, in season one, killed infected Regis 753 passenger Joan before she could attack her own children. Though some fans of the books assumed this was the first appearance of pivotal Sun Hunter character Quinlan, it was an intentional misdirect on the part of the writers. It was actually a new vampire created for the series named Vaun, a protégé of Quinlan's. "Vaun needed to be a guy in action before Quinlan, so Quinlan could be introduced more like a trainer or sensei," says del Toro.

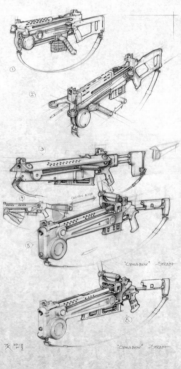

ABOVE Sun Hunter glove designs by Guy Davis.

TOP RIGHT Early Quinlan concept art by Guy Davis.

RIGHT Costume design concepts for Sun Hunters by Guy Davis.

FAR RIGHT Sun Hunter gun concepts by Bartol Rendulic.

TOP LEFT Costume design for Sun Hunter Quinlan by Guy Davis.
ABOVE Sun Hunter mask variations by Guy Davis.
BOTTOM LEFT Quinlan sword concepts by Shaun Martens.
BELOW Quinlan concept art by Guy Davis.

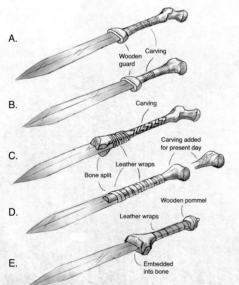

A.

Carving
Wooden guard

B.

Carving

C.

Carving added for present day
Leather wraps
Bone split

D.

Wooden pommel
Leather wraps

E.

Embedded into bone

When Quinlan arrived, played by stage-trained actor Rupert Penry-Jones, he immediately set himself apart as a character not to be trifled with, attired in spiked, lug-sole boots, red-and-black gauntlets, and a floor-length double-breasted coat with a pin featuring a dragon chasing its tail. "He's half human, half vampire," says Chuck Hogan. "Of course, from a human perspective, you're all vampire. Half is as good as being 100 percent. But he's completely motivated by an ancient grudge to go after The Master. So Quinlan is begrudgingly on the side of the humans."

Quinlan's history, revealed in a flashback to ancient Rome where he's a fierce gladiator freed by an admiring senator, suggests a level of combat experience unsurpassed by vampires or humans. "He's somebody who's seen a lot," says Carlton Cuse. "He's aware of mankind's ability to be horrible and cruel apart from the existence of monsters. He knows that in the right circumstances, humans are capable of very dark things. It's a relevant attitude, because the world of season two couldn't exist without a human population that looked the other way. He's a tragic figure in a way. For him, immortality is more curse than blessing."

OPPOSITE Sun Hunter Quinlan (Rupert Penry-Jones) was once a gladiator, as revealed in the season two episode "The Born."

ABOVE Swords rendered by Chris Penna and branding designs created for Quinlan.

TOP RIGHT Period artwork created for the Ancient Rome flashback sequences in "The Born."

RIGHT Setrakian (David Bradley) and Quinlan (Penry-Jones) team up to fight The Master in season two.

Along with fleshing out the strigoi ranks, season two also introduces Staten Island councilwoman Justine Faraldo, played by Samantha Mathis. Faraldo takes matters into her own hands regarding the spreading vampire threat, suspending the democratic process, assembling her own force, and curbing citizens' freedom as a result. But when it works in her district, she becomes beloved and aligns with the vampire hunters to make Red Hook safe. As Carlton Cuse describes her, Faraldo is "rooted in the tradition of working-class New Yorkers, total salt of the earth, without pretense, trying to do good in the best possible way she can." Yet when her success brings her power, it becomes apparent that Faraldo's intentions may not be entirely altruistic. To Cuse's thinking, Faraldo is the political embodiment of the question, What would you sacrifice to ensure

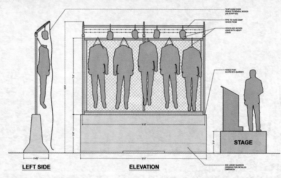

your survival? "What are the consequences of giving up that personal liberty?" he muses. "Is it worth doing that for the greater good? For us, there are a lot of metaphors to what happened in Europe in the 1930s, when there was a lot of economic turmoil, depression, social disorder, and out of this rose leaders who promised to make things better. People bought into their promise when the cost was freedom and democracy."

Along with Justine, season two marks the debut of another significant new female character (who, like Justine, was created just for the series): Coco Marchand, an ex-model who becomes Eldritch Palmer's assistant. With a rift growing between Palmer and Eichhorst as both vie for The Master's attention, Coco—played by Lizzie Brochere—becomes a key ally for Palmer, professionally and personally. Says producer J. Miles Dale, "This gorgeous younger woman softens him up, and since Palmer's always been sick and never had love, it becomes a new color for him. Lizzie's a great actress, too, so she was a fun addition."

TOP AND MIDDLE RIGHT From the episode "Fort Defiance," a gruesome display of beheaded strigoi as a show of anti-vampire strength.

CENTER Art department outline of the hanging strigoi, by Chris Penna.

FAR LEFT Councilwoman Justine Faraldo (Samantha Mathis).

ABOVE Eldritch Palmer (Jonathan Hyde) falls for his assistant, Coco Marchand (Lizzie Brochere).

OPPOSITE LEFT Former wrestler Angel (Joaquin Cosio) helps Gus (Miguel Gomez) form an army for Quinlan in the episode "Fallen Light."

OPPOSITE TOP RIGHT Castle art for the luchador movie scene that appears in the episode "The Silver Angel," rendered by Chris Penna.

Season two also introduces one of del Toro's prized creations from *The Fall*, the second book in *The Strain* trilogy. Angel is a masked Mexican wrestler who, despite being way past his glory days, becomes an important figure in the battle against the strigoi. In many ways, Angel—played by Joaquin Cosio—is del Toro's favorite character, since he represents the luchador movies of his childhood, in which masked strongmen battled everything from aliens to Nazis and, yes, even vampires. "I created him without telling Chuck, just the way he created Fet without telling me!" says del Toro. "By the time I'd run it past him, it was too late. He was already in the book!"

Angel's introduction to the show allowed del Toro to realize a lifelong dream and re-create an old luchador movie. Seizing the opportunity, he directed the prologue to Angel's debut episode, a four-minute segment designed to look like a vintage black-and-white Mexican wrestler movie. Del Toro's segment comes complete with span-dex-clad, leather-masked antagonists in boxing boots—the Silver Angel (the young version of our hero) versus the Dark Lord—and bikini-clad vampire women with cone bras, capelets, and Elvis collars. J. Miles Dale, who directed the rest of the episode, couldn't believe Guillermo was so adamant about helming the intro sequence: "He was, like, 'I have to do it. I can never go home to Mexico if I don't. I'll beg you!' I just started laughing. Here I sit with Guillermo del Toro, and he's begging *me* to shoot second unit on my episode!"

For del Toro, though, often it's second-unit sequences—typically focused on shots that don't feature the primary actors—that speak to his vast imagination. "Any time I can support an episode with a bit of second-unit work is fun for me," he says, "because second unit actually gets all the fun shots."

THE FEELERS

SEASON TWO SEES THE DEBUT OF one of del Toro's and Hogan's creepier inventions: the blind strigoi children known as the Feelers. Created by The Master, they emerge from a loamy pit of dirt in an abandoned soap factory and become the eerie charges of Kelly Goodweather, now on the path to full vampirism and on the hunt for her son, Jack.

"I think it's great that Kelly has this brood of children she's using to help her," says Chuck Hogan. "They're children brought before The Master, who turns each one, and because they are blind, he is able to heighten their other senses in the afterlife, like smell and hearing." Since the turning process takes time—with stung victims often retreating into a hiding place to transform—these blind children need a safe place to develop: "So the Feelers go into this nursery of grave-like soil," says Hogan.

They communicate with Kelly through a language of clicks, but as with any team-picking scenario, not every Feeler makes the cut, with Kelly brutally dismissing the weaker also-rans by snapping their necks. The chosen become a loyal squad, though, in Kelly's search for her son.

"The Feelers were a big addition, because we were all about upping the game in this season," says Carlton Cuse. "Part of what I love about the show is the expansive mythology, with multiple forces of antagonism in the storyline. There are different types of vampires with different powers, different levels of sentience, and there's a whole rich, detailed, and fantastic backstory to their mythology. I personally love the Feelers."

The Feelers also allow actress Natalie Brown—originally introduced as a regular mom embroiled in a custody battle with Eph—to blossom into one of the show's most potent vampire warriors. "Natalie is one of the great discoveries of the show," says Cuse. "We cast her because she was this wonderful actress who could give us a nuanced performance as Eph's wife. But the truth is she's a spectacular vampire."

Kelly turns at a slower rate than other victims because the creators felt that, as she started as a human we cared about, there needed to be some residual sympathy for her as her change materialized. (This is reflected in the second season

PREVIOUS PAGES Guillermo del Toro directing the black-and-white luchador movie excerpt.

OPPOSITE Kelly Goodweather (Natalie Brown) overseeing a pair of Feelers.

ABOVE Illustration of the Feelers' pit by Juan Pablo Garcia Tames.

storyline that has Eichhorst helping Kelly create a more human appearance for herself, much as he does in the mirror each day with prosthetic pieces.) So while Kelly continues to affect a gaunt appearance with sunken eyes and thinning hair, the makeup department needed to ensure we still saw Natalie Brown in there somewhere as she developed her maternal connection to the Feelers. "Natalie's a huge secret weapon for us," says Hogan. "You really feel her weird vampire affection for these creatures."

As for the Feelers themselves, they had to make an instant impact when rising as a horde from their vampire incubator. Their entrance was filmed at a real disused soap factory that in the story is purchased by Stoneheart. "What attracted us to it was the textures of the walls, which had this crusty detergent all over [them]," says production designer Tamara Deverell. "It had an incredibly

ghost-like, strange feel to it." Deverell built the Feelers' concrete, dirt-filled nursery pen beneath a two-story-high funnel on the factory's main floor that had been used to fill bins with detergents. "The pit looked like it belonged there," says Deverell. "We put railings around it, and a kind of gooey green cesspool leading up to it. Then we put some lights below it to give it this strange glow."

Casting the Feelers was the next step. Having had success hiring dancers as vampire extras, producer J. Miles Dale and choreographer Roberto Campanella sought similarly flexible kids to play the Feelers. "We talked about how they might move, and I said, 'Let's see if we can get the Feelers to run around like crabs,'" recalls Dale. "So we reached out to gymnasts and held workshops to

see how these kids could move. We came up with a pretty cool language for them. So they look weird; they crab around and nuzzle with Kelly. It's kind of unsettling."

The ten most long-limbed and limber children were selected and then given a vampire-stage-three treatment from the makeup/prosthetics department—thinning hair, ghoulishly pale skin—but with some slight differences around the eyes. Says creature shop guru Steve Newburn, "At one point, Guillermo del Toro drew a Feeler doodle on the table, and it looked like the eyes were burned, radiating out, so there were these little white eyes in the middle of these black areas. It was really piercing. So we settled on a traditional white eye, surrounded by all this black and brown, almost like scarring. It almost looked like a bandit's mask, and it made the eyes really pop."

For the most part, this shiver-inducing clique of spider-walking minors was created as a practical effect: trained kids performing in front of a camera. But occasionally, for wide shots of Feelers scurrying up walls and across ceilings or dodging gunfire, digital doubles were used. The visual effects team at Mr. X, headed by Dennis Berardi and on-set

supervisor Matt Glover, took full photo scans of performers that were prominently featured and then built digital versions of each. These digital models would then be animated individually, rather than creating one generic Feeler that would be modified over and over again. Photo surveys of all the sets allowed the digital artists to accurately place their CGI Feelers into the scene. Once the artists at Mr. X got a shot to specifications they liked, del Toro would give his feedback on the shot, addressing the realism of its gravity or giving environmental suggestions—Might a Feeler running down the side of an old church dislodge some dust?—to help make the sequence as realistic as possible.

Digital effects were only a last resort, though, and sometimes old-school camera tricks were the best solution. A shot of a Feeler crawling across a building's window, for instance, could be captured using a pane of glass level with the floor and a camera below pointing up. "We'd shoot from underneath looking straight up onto some glass, then have one of the children scurry across the glass," says Glover. "Then, when you composite the shot sideways [adding in a digital background], it looks like they're climbing [up a] window."

OPPOSITE LEFT Actors playing Feelers, the infected minions of Kelly Goodweather (Natalie Brown).

OPPOSITE RIGHT Kelly (Brown) with two of the Feelers who move along the ground in an eerie shuffle and communicate through sharp, chittering sounds.

TOP LEFT AND BOTTOM LEFT Before and after shots show how digital doubles were used for the Feelers in certain scenes.

ABOVE An actor portrays one of the Feelers wearing green trousers so that the VFX team at Mr. X can remove the lower torso of the character in post-production and add grisly entrails.

MASTER TRANSFER

THE ORIGINAL *THE STRAIN* NOVEL revealed a rich backstory for The Master. While this flashback didn't fit within the narrative of season one, the opening of season two presented the perfect opportunity to realize this fan-favorite part of *The Strain*'s lore. Guillermo del Toro was on hand to direct this sequence, the opener to the first episode of the season, which reveals how The Master facilitates his unique brand of immortality by switching from one body to another. Says Chuck Hogan, "We thought it was a great way to start off season two: to show him becoming himself but, at the same time, unbeknownst to the viewer, slyly plant the seed for another switch halfway through the season." Jusef Sardu is a tall Albanian nobleman on a hunting expedition in the Carpathian Mountains when his family is mysteriously slaughtered. Venturing into a cave to find the source of this butchery, he comes across a gaunt, freakish creature gnawing on his brother. Grabbing Sardu, The Master projectile vomits a torrent of worms from his engorged wattle into the mouth of his new host body.

"The process is just super cool," says Carlton Cuse. "It's one of those things I really love about Guillermo. He has this amazing ability to invent

wonderful, unique genre moments that really resonate."

The way that The Master controls the dissemination of his worms is a concept del Toro considers essential to the story's mythology. It's a variation on a characteristic found in rattlesnakes. "The younger the rattlesnake, the less efficient it is at attacking," says del Toro. "An older rattlesnake bites you and graduates how much venom it can put into you, whereas a young rattlesnake empties its venom glands on every bite. So The Master can control very deviously how many worms go into each of his victims." In Jusef Sardu's case, it's a full-on worm transfusion.

Del Toro directed the cave scene in a specially created set with the imposing Robert Maillet getting the chance to appear on camera without the extensive prosthetics he wore in season one as the most recent version of The Master. Doug Jones (*Pan's Labyrinth*, *Hellboy*), a favorite of del Toro who also stars as one of The Ancients, appears in the scene as the wraithlike, pre-Sardu Master. Maillet was dressed in a lace wig of long, flowing black locks hand-tied by a member of the hair department, and outfitted in a non-tattered version of his season one The Master cape, built by costume

designer Luis Sequeira. Jones, however, underwent a more considerable preparation: a full head-to-toe prosthetic makeup, the application of which took five hours. "Every single inch of his body was covered in pieces, because his character was completely naked," says creature shop supervisor Steve Newburn. "It was two feet, two legs, a pair of tight shorts, a front torso, a back torso, arms, hands, a neck and back of head, face, chin, and ears. All very veiny, with a grey skin tone."

The thinking behind this volume of prosthetic pieces was that Jones's portrayal of The Master would be very movement-oriented, involving

OPPOSITE TOP LEFT Keyframe art of Jusef Sardu encountering The Master by Francisco Ruiz Velasco.

OPPOSITE RIGHT, TOP AND BOTTOM Jusef Sardu costume concepts by Keith Thompson.

TOP LEFT Pre-Master Sardu with village children, art by Juan Pablo Garcia Tames.

TOP RIGHT The infected Sardu at night in the village, art by Juan Pablo Garcia Tames.

ABOVE Sardu encountering The Master in a cave, art by Juan Pablo Garcia Tames.

RIGHT The Master in Sardu's cloaked body, art by Chris Penna.

Producer J. Miles Dale has nothing but praise for Jones's brief, memorable Master turn. "He did a kickass job on the pre-Sardu Master," says Dale. "He's in a league of his own with that kind of stuff."

Digital effects were used to complete the worm-transfer shots, the final images so breathtakingly disturbing that there was concern that they may have to be toned down for broadcast. Visual effects supervisor Matt Glover of Mr. X, who was on set to collect information on camera movement, lighting, and staging, says del Toro knew from the start it would be an extreme moment. "This wasn't a case where we started small and finally got there," says Glover. "It was always going to be over-the-top, go for the throat."

To augment the scene between the two actors, the effects team needed to insert a handful of computer-generated components: a re-created wattle on Doug Jones's Master; the river of white, worm-laden goo landing all over Sardu; plus a bunch of individually animated worms that have a life of their own. "These are the worms you see explicitly penetrating his skin, curling over and diving in, basically," says Glover. "Many are going straight into his mouth, but we've also got a layer of 'hero' ones going in through the corner of his eyes, burrowing into his face, nose. It's like what we did with a single worm on Kelly in season one, going into her eye. It's that but on a grand scale."

The rest of the prologue features Maillet's Sardu transforming as he returns to his village, his skin sinking in and his hair falling out. Ironically, Maillet endured a longer makeup process for this scene than when being readied as the final version of The Master. "We'd streamlined his The Master process so much we'd gotten it down to an hour and forty-five minutes," says Newburn. "But here, because he retained many of his own features, all the appliances were extremely thin, and every edge had to be perfect. This was actually a more elaborate makeup and took about four hours to do. [When it was finished], he looked like a ghoul. It's your first hint of things to come."

As the prologue gives way to present day, The Master is revealed to be a wounded, badly burned creature following his exposure to the sun when escaping Setrakian's attack at the end of season one. This is the setup for one of the second season's most significant events: the Sardu version of The Master transferring into Bolivar's body.

This time around Newburn and his crew had to create what they called the "Burn Master," a full nude body for Maillet that showed the extent of the sun-scarring damage. It meant sculpting a new head, new hands, and other body pieces, which were treated to what Newburn calls "a lymphatic-colored, orangey-brown jelly that just looked nasty when you see him briefly in the shadows." When the Master's cloak is eventually removed, the disfiguring marks of "worm trails," as del Toro refers to them, are also visible. These are the scarring marks left behind when the worms inside The Master stop moving around and settle. "We painted him head to toe in those trails," says Newburn. "All the ornamentation you see sculpted into his cheeks and temples? Well, they're all over his body too."

crawling around on all fours and crouching on his taloned, bat-like feet. A full-body suit pulled over the actor would have likely restricted Jones's ability to get the most out of his entirely physical performance. "Suits just don't move well," says Newburn. "And because this was only going to happen once, we glued him head to toe in appliances. No body paint. Believe me, if he'd been featured twenty more times like this, we'd have reconsidered." The effect was to get a hybrid creature of sorts. "It's one of our vampires crossed with a hundred-year-old man, crossed with a skin-and-bones concentration camp victim. He's a full-blown corpse."

OPPOSITE From the episode "BK, NY," The Master (Doug Jones) transfers a torrent of bloodworms onto and into Jusef Sardu (Robert Maillet).

ABOVE Digital effects added the stinger to the pre-Sardu Master (Jones).

RIGHT From the season one finale, a sun-stricken Master flees from a confrontation with Setrakian.

Mr. X handled the aspects of the Burn Master that couldn't be applied to an actor—namely, what's beneath the character's burned-away flesh. "Half his face is more or less missing, and you can see inner structure," says Glover. "One of his eye sockets is completely burnt away, and you can see the whole sphere of his eye, and the cheekbone around his eye socket. When he talks, you can see right through to his teeth moving around. But also, he's just full of worms, which ties into the transfer. You can see them burrowing in and out. It drives home the biology they're setting up."

Once the hobbled Master vacates his host body to take over Bolivar, a new costume had to be created to signify a renewed, strengthened vampire kingpin. Costume designer Luis Sequeira fashioned a full-length black leather coat reminiscent of Cossack priests, but with one key difference that ties into Bolivar's color scheme. "We added five slits running down the back and sides, lined in red," says Sequeira. "When he's walking, everything lays flat against each other, but when he starts twirling to fight, the cloak splits apart, and you see all the red. We had fun with that one."

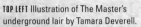

LIGHT READING

MAKING *THE LUMEN*

ONE OF THE CENTRAL STORYLINES in *The Fall* is the search for the *Occido Lumen*, an ancient, mystical book that contains information that may hold the key to subverting The Master's plans and ending the vampire apocalypse. When Setrakian learns that this tome is actually in New York, he steps up his efforts to find it. Needless to say, the forces of evil are after it also, which eventually leads to a tense auction for the manuscript held at the church headquarters of canny gangster Alonso Creem (Jamie Hector), who's turned his criminal enterprise—introduced briefly in Gus's season one storyline—into a black market business capitalizing on society's downfall. "The stakes couldn't be higher," says Carlton Cuse. "Since Setrakian and Eichhorst both want the Lumen at all costs, it felt like a tremendously good narrative endpoint for our season."

Since the book's reveal is such a key moment in the story, creating a realistic prop of perceptible gravitas and physical heft was essential. Production designer Tamara Deverell and illustrators Juan Pablo Garcia Tames and Chris Penna began with considerable research into ancient texts and symbology. They also used the original novels for image reference. In designing the cover, Deverell and Tames blended images, symbols, and lettering—some from antiquity, such as a two-headed gryphon, and others newly created, such as a hand with two arrows. The ever-present biohazard symbol was also incorporated subtly, per del Toro's direction. This design was then

grafted onto a mock-up foam core box so they could get feedback from del Toro and Cuse on not just the cover art but the *Lumen*'s size.

Once approved, a draft of the correctly sized cover illustration was handed over to creature shop supervisor Steve Newburn and his crew, who sculpted the cover and spine. A base pattern was first created out of styrene, after which a mold and castings were made. The final casting was urethane resin, which was then treated to an aging process that gave the exterior of the book a pounded metal look. Final touches included detailed silver-leaf application and further aging with tar.

ABOVE Concept art of the *Occido Lumen* as seen from various angles by Juan Pablo Garcia Tames.

TOP RIGHT AND RIGHT Drawings for the inside of the *Occido Lumen* by Juan Pablo Garcia Tames and Chris Penna.

OPPOSITE The final *Occido Lumen* prop on set.

The *Lumen*'s contents were an even more painstaking affair, pages and pages of text and illustration that needed to look like a centuries-old tome, a prized relic from the early years of printed material. An initial set of pages was created using woodcuts, one of the oldest methods for printing, followed by a second set that suggested a classic illuminated manuscript, full of colorful lettering and ornate decoration and borders. (A gold marker pen was used to achieve a gold-leaf effect.) Tames and Penna crafted those illustrations using a combination of images taken directly from ancient books but tweaked for the show's purposes—a medieval drawing of a witch, perhaps, augmented by a projected stinger. They also used references taken directly from descriptions in the *Strain* novels. These from-scratch drawings included a pair of pages that each showcases a human figure with six wings: one cloaked in black, the other in front of a Star of David. The cloaked figure illustration would feature prominently in season two as a photocopied page from the *Lumen* carried around by Setrakian as proof the book exists and something with which to verify the *Lumen* once found.

THESE PAGES *Lumen* pages drawn by Juan Pablo Garcia Tames and Chris Penna.

Kampf der Vampire und der Engel

Lamashtu istein historisch älteren Bild, das eine Markierung an der Figur der Lilith verlassen. Viele Beschwörungen ihr berufen als böswillige "Tochter des Himmels" oder von Anu , und sie wird oft als eine erschreckende blutsaugende Kreatur mit einem Löwen dargestellt Kopf und der Körper eines Esels. Ähnlich wie Lilitu, Lamashtu vor allem bei Neugeborenen und ihren Mttern gejagt. Sie wurde gesagt, um schwangere Frauen aufmerksam zu beobachten, vor allem, wenn sie in den Arbeitsmarkt ging. Danach sie das Neugeborene von der Mutter zu entreien wrde

LEGENDS OF VAMP IRE SIND SEIL JA VRTAUSENDEN EX ISTIERT Einheiten berwi egend als Vampire

Vampire die torchured

Heute wissen wir, diese Einheiten berwieg end als Vampire, aber in den alten Zeiten, der Begriff Vampir gab es nicht; Blut trinken und ähnliche Aktivitäten wurden zug~ eschrieben Dämonen oder Geister , die Fleisch essen wrde und Blut trinken; selbst der Teufel wurde als Synonym fr den Vampir. Fast jede Nation verbunden Blut trinken mit einer Art Wie~ dergänger oder Dämon, der Ghouls von Arabien ,

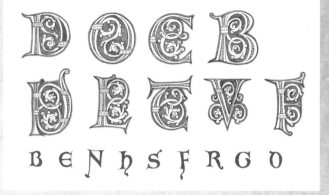

BENHSFRGD

Einige der häu~ figsten Ur~ sachen des Vampirismus in slawischen Folklore ge~ hören, ein Zauberer oder eine unmoralische Person; Leiden einer "unnatrlich" oder frhen Tod wie Selbstmord; Erkom~ munikation ; unsachgemäe Be~ stattungsrituale; ein Tier, Springen oder ein Vogel fliegen ber der Leiche oder dem leeren Grab (in serbischer Volks~

Die malaysische Penanggalan kann entweder eine schöne alte oder junge Frau, die ihre Schönheit durch die aktive Nut~ zung der erhaltenen schwarzen Magie oder andere unnatrliche Mittel und wird in der Regel in der lokalen Folklore beschrie~ ben dunkel oder dämonische Natur zu sein.

Sie ist in der Lage, ihre fanged Kopf, der in der Nacht herum fliegt auf der Suche nach Blut, in der Regel von schwangeren Frauen, zu lösen. Malaysier

Argentum

Füttern gejagt. Sie wurde gesagt, um schwangere Frauen aufmerksam zu beobachten, vor allem, wenn sie in den Arbeitsmarkt ging. Danach sie

Layouts of the illustrations, with Old German text added, were created in a computer, then sent to the printing company Idodat, which specializes in paper props for movies and television. Idodat calligraphers meticulously hand lettered the text for the pages, scanned them, printed out the *Lumen* pages onto parchment, and then aged it to appear slightly stiff. The whole *Lumen*—which measured 12 inches long by 8 inches wide and was two-and-a-half inches thick and filled with plenty of blank pages to pad it out—was then handed to a bookbinder for hand-sewing. Once the finished *Lumen* came back from the bookbinder, the team did a final pass on the illumination, hand painting, and calligraphy.

All in all, creating the show's one and only *Lumen* took months of work, the price for creating an artifact that is of unquantifiable valuable to *The Strain*'s characters, both good and evil. "It's the prop to end all props," says producer J. Miles Dale. "I don't know how many thousands of man hours there are in that book, but it was crazy. That was a big one."

OPPOSITE *Lumen* pages drawn by Juan Pablo Garcia Tames and Chris Penna.

ABOVE Fet and Setrakian try to buy the *Lumen* from gangster Alonso Creem (Jamie Hector).

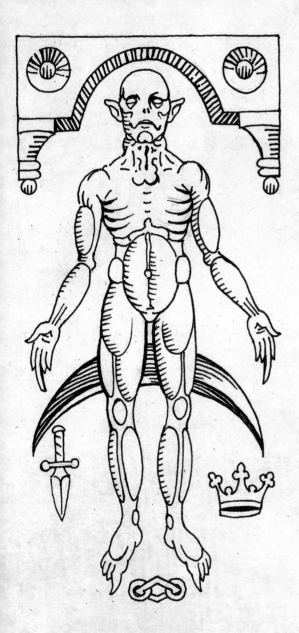

OPPOSITE Design for *The Strain* crew jacket by Guy Davis.

ABOVE Illustration for the *Lumen* by Juan Pablo Garcia Tames and Chris Penna.

TOP RIGHT Setrakian, Dutch, Zack, and Eph will face even greater threats as *The Strain* continues.

FOLLOWING PAGES Illustrations for Silver Angel movie posters by Juan Pablo Garcia Tames.

CONCLUSION

SO FAR, OVER TWO THRILLING SEASONS, *The Strain* has unveiled its nightmare scenario with a meticulous eye for the ways good people struggle in the fight to thwart evil. Triumph and tragedy intertwine. Short-sightedness has long-ranging implications. The will to survive battles the desire to do what's right. Alliances form but, in the process, threaten bonds elsewhere. To face the darkness that threatens you is to, unfortunately, engage that darkness. How can one not come away unscathed?

These themes account for the special sinister grip of *The Strain* for they expose without any pretense the characteristic of vampires that scares us most: that they will irrevocably change us. The strigoi that sprung from Guillermo del Toro's imagination are fierce and ravenous creatures who bring with them total societal breakdown and the threat of bodily invasion. Whether the human beings in their sights succumb to them or stand their ground and fight, they invariably change.

"The vampire figure in English literature was born with the ambivalence of being a seductive image or a monstrous creature," says del Toro. "Bram Stoker was dealing with one of the most repressed, regimented societies in the history of mankind—Victorian England—where the hint of impropriety was enough to cause a blush, raise eyebrows, or cause social disgrace. Well, we may not believe we are, but we are an incredibly morally fragile society that thinks of itself as good and just, but in reality this belief is paper-thin. We're close to being Neanderthals, you know? The same way that Count Dracula came to Victorian England, turning people completely brutal and savage in their war against him, that's the effect The Master would have in our society."

"He pushes the most basic buttons of mammalian antagonism—even reptilian antagonism," adds del Toro. "When a force that primal hits you, it transforms you."

These past few years, *The Strain* has given birth to its own artistic mutations in the journey from page to screen, as del Toro's and Chuck Hogan's words have inspired a gifted team of creators to turn an ambitiously conceived vampire scourge into bold and spellbinding television. Though it's a fraught road ahead for the show's dauntless strigoi hunters, future seasons of *The Strain* promise fans ever more strange, wicked, and majestically horrific pleasures.

TITAN BOOKS

A division of Titan Publishing Group Ltd
144 Southwark Street
London SE1 0UP
www.titanbooks.com

Find us on Facebook: www.facebook.com/TitanBooks
Follow us on Twitter: @TitanBooks

Published by Titan Books, London, in 2016.

A CIP catalogue record for this title is available from the British Library.

Published by arrangement with Insight Editions
PO Box 3088, San Rafael, CA 94912, USA
www.insighteditions.com

ISBN: 9781783299645

PUBLISHER: Raoul Goff
ACQUISITIONS MANAGER: Robbie Schmidt
EXECUTIVE EDITOR: Vanessa Lopez
PROJECT EDITOR: Chris Prince
PRODUCTION EDITOR: Rachel Anderson
EDITORIAL ASSISTANT: Gregory Solano
ART DIRECTOR: Chrissy Kwasnik
DESIGNER: Jon Glick
PRODUCTION MANAGER: Blake Mitchum
JUNIOR PRODUCTION MANAGER: Alix Nicholaeff

Insight Editions would like to thank Guillermo del Toro, Carlton Cuse, Chuck Hogan,
Gary Ungar, Ian Gibson, Josh Izzo, Nicole Spiegel, Guy Davis, Tamara Deverell,
Spencer Cushing, Luke Groves, Chloe Moffet, Cory Bird, and Gregg Nations.

THIS PAGE Bolivar's tattoo, illustration by Bartol Rendulic.

PAGES 16, 17, AND 18 *The Strain* comic art courtesy Dark Horse Comics.

The Strain and *The Strain: Night Eternal* comic books first published by Dark Horse Comics Inc.

ROOTS of PEACE   REPLANTED PAPER

Insight Editions, in association with Roots of Peace, will plant two trees for each
tree used in the manufacturing of this book. Roots of Peace is an internationally
renowned humanitarian organization dedicated to eradicating land mines worldwide
and converting war-torn lands into productive farms and wildlife habitats. Roots of
Peace will plant two million fruit and nut trees in Afghanistan and provide farmers
there with the skills and support necessary for sustainable land use.

Manufactured in China by Insight Editions

10 9 8 7 6 5 4 3 2 1

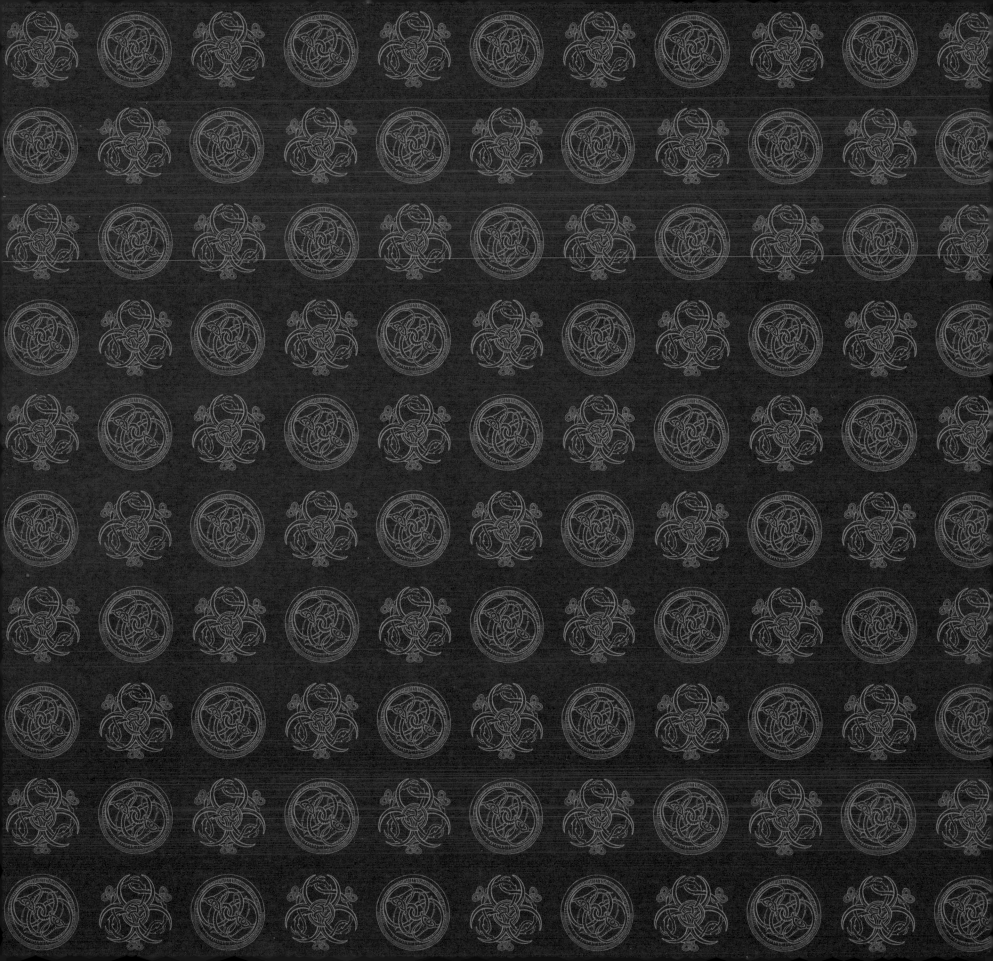